WHAT PEOPLE ARE SAYING ABOUT

Ingredients

THE COOKBOOK THAT'S IN
MILLIONS OF HOMES WORLDWIDE!

"[Kim and Rachael's] talent for devising cheap meals is impressive."

—*The Washington Post*

"Perfect for a busy night when you don't feel like cooking, but want something good."

—*The Parkersburg News and Sentinel* (W.Va.)

"From the perspective of a busy mom who is looking for an alternative over frozen and fast foods, *4 Ingredients* has got it going on!"

—What's That Smell? (blog)

"*4 Ingredients* has fast, palate-pleasing meals for every family occasion, including lunch-box meals for the kids."

—Chef Mom, SheKnows.com (blog)

"This book is a wonderful source of inspiration but also that clean slate so many of us are looking for in preparing family meals."

—ModernMom (blog)

"I love that this book strips it down and focuses on the joy of simple cooking. And simple cooking that tastes wonderful."

—Kansas City Mamas (blog)

"Making these meals less complicated also includes making them easier to prep and clean up afterwards and giving you more time to spend with your family doing what you love."

—Baby Dickey (blog)

"The best part? Oh, that's easy—being able to put something amazing on the dinner table and not having to break the bank buying ingredients!"

—Misadventures in Baby Raising (blog)

"*4 Ingredients* is one of those books that will never be put away because it's such a useful book!"

—Living Mi Vida Loca (blog)

"Kim and Rachael have found some great ways to use common grocery store ingredients to create quick and tasty household meals!"

—Dashing for Deals (blog)

"This cookbook is right up my alley!"

—Retail Therapy Lounge (blog)

"The recipes are all straightforward and easy to understand."

—From Val's Kitchen (blog)

"*4 Ingredients* is perfect for the busy, budget-conscious cook."

—Masshole Mommy (blog)

"The *4 Ingredients* cookbook is an invaluable resource in the kitchen."

—Minnesota Mama's Must-Haves (blog)

4 Ingredients is also available as an ebook.

Ingredients

More Than 400 Quick, Easy, and Delicious Recipes Using 4 or Fewer Ingredients

· ·

Kim McCosker and Rachael Bermingham

ATRIA PAPERBACK

New York   London   Toronto   Sydney   New Delhi

ATRIA PAPERBACK
A Division of Simon & Schuster, Inc.
1230 Avenue of the Americas
New York, NY 10020

First Atria Paperback edition February 2012

ATRIA PAPERBACK and colophon are trademarks of Simon & Schuster, Inc.

For information about special discounts for bulk purchases, please contact Simon & Schuster Special Sales at 1-866-506-1949 or business@simonandschuster.com.

The Simon & Schuster Speakers Bureau can bring authors to your live event. For more information or to book an event, contact the Simon & Schuster Speakers Bureau at 1-866-248-3049 or visit our website at www.simonspeakers.com.

Designed by Lisa Stokes

Manufactured in the United States of America

10   9   8   7   6   5   4   3   2   1

The Library of Congress has cataloged the hardcover edition as follows:

McCosker, Kim.
    4 ingredients : more than 400 quick, easy, and delicious recipes using 4 or fewer ingredients / Kim McCosker, Rachael Bermingham.
        p.   cm.
    Includes index.
    1. Quick and easy cooking.   2. Cookbooks.   I. Bermingham, Rachael.   II. Title.
III. Title: Four ingredients.
    TX833.5.M428   2012
    641.5'55—dc22   2011002926

ISBN 978-1-4516-3514-0
ISBN 978-1-4516-3515-7 (pbk)
ISBN 978-1-4516-3516-4 (ebook)

CONTENTS

INTRODUCTION

Have you ever experienced any of the following?

1. You look at your watch and think, "Gosh, it's 6:30! What am I going to cook for dinner?"
2. You collect your children from school and immediately hear a resounding "I'm hungry!" from the backseat.
3. You spend hours on the phone trying to explain how to cook something to your grown child who has just moved out.
4. OH MY GOD . . . They're coming over for dinner!!!?
5. The clock says 11 p.m. and you're exhausted, but the kids' lunch boxes must be packed for the next day. Peanut butter and jelly? Again?
6. You go to the pantry, look at it (full to the brim), and think, "Nothing in there!"
7. You find yourself cooking spaghetti and meatballs for the kids AGAIN!!!
8. You spend all afternoon cooking, only to have to scour the kitchen afterward.
9. You want to make something memorable for a dinner party but dread having to buy and prepare so many ingredients.
10. You feel excited about cooking great food but want to do it without breaking the weekly food budget.

WELL, THIS BOOK IS FOR YOU!

And your family, your friends, and their families and their friends.

The *4 Ingredients* concept is all about preparing delicious food easily and inexpensively by:

Reducing the number of ingredients required to make something yummy. Every one of these fabulous recipes is made with only four or fewer ingredients. Our aim was to simplify without compromising on flavor.

Reducing the number of utensils required to make something yummy. The only measuring equipment required to make the recipes in this book is a set of measuring spoons and a measuring cup. Any other measurements (e.g., ounces) will be marked on the store-bought product.

Reducing the amount of money spent on food each week. Food is one of the largest items in the weekly budget, so it is well worth shopping around for good-quality food at a reasonable price. By reducing the ingredients, you do not need to buy as much. A recipe with eight ingredients generally costs more to prepare than a recipe with four.

Reducing the mess. By simplifying the recipe, you often simplify the cleanup, which adds up to saved time . . . something most of us could do with more of these days.

We are two everyday moms who absolutely love and adore our families, and like most busy mothers are always appreciative of ways to create more time for them.

The reality of *4 Ingredients* began when Rachael Bermingham presented Kim McCosker with a signed copy of her new book *Read My Lips*. Kim was admiring what her extremely talented friend had achieved when Rachael remarked, "Everyone has a good book inside them!" And a little while later the very courageous and creative Mrs. McCosker validated that statement by casually mentioning her own book idea to Rachael.

"What is it?" Rach asked.

"A book full of yummy recipes with four or fewer ingredients."

"BRILLIANT!" Rachael exclaimed. "You HAVE to do it!"

"Too hard, no time," Kim replied.

"No way," said the unstoppable Mrs. Bermingham.

"Love . . . I've had this idea for years. I've been collecting recipes for years and have never done anything with it. I'll sit on it for years more because the mere thought of writing a book is SCARIER than a teething toddler . . . AND THEY ARE SCARY!!!" (We both currently have them.)

"It's not that hard," Rach said.

And Kim replied, "Yeah . . . you write it with me, then!!!!"

We self-published *4 Ingredients* in our native Australia in 2007. What began as a revolutionary idea hatched in Kim's kitchen has since become a necessity in homes all over the country. Literally millions of copies have been sold. Currently, one out of ten Australian households has a copy of *4 Ingredients*! And now we're thrilled to be able to share this wonderful, time-saving, money-saving concept with the United States. In the past three years, we have come up with even more delicious recipes we know you'll love, including Huevos Rancheros, Coney Island Burgers, and Sweet Potato Mash with Crisp Sage Leaves—all with fewer than four ingredients. For this edition, we also took out dishes that are, perhaps, a bit *too* Aussie, even for those of you who have traveled to the glorious Down Under. We'll save the Vegemite for the second book!

Best wishes and happy cooking!

—Rachael and Kim, December 2010

IN THE CUPBOARD

4 Ingredients offers a wide range of delicious recipes, cooked for our families and friends for many a barbecue, party, Sunday dinner, Friday drinks get-together, and so on. In all our trials, there seemed to be a bunch of staple ingredients we always called upon. What we aim to do in this section is help you stock your kitchen pantry with those basic ingredients that will help you make and flavor your dishes—and save many a dish from disaster.

Please note: In this book we have not included salt, pepper, and water as part of the 4 Ingredients.

SAVORY	SWEET
Barbecue sauce	All-purpose and self-rising flour
Beef and chicken bouillon cubes	Bamboo skewers
Bread crumbs	Canned fruit: pineapple, pear
Curry powder	Cinnamon
Dijon mustard	Coconut, shredded
French onion soup (dry mix)	Condensed milk
Fresh vegetables	Cornstarch
Garlic	Cream
Ketchup	Cream cheese
Lemons	Eggs
Mayonnaise	Evaporated milk
Minced ginger	Food coloring
Peppercorns	Fresh fruit
Pesto	Gelatin

SAVORY	SWEET
Pine nuts	Graham crackers
Refrigerated piecrusts	Honey
Rice	Jams: apricot, strawberry, etc.
Sea salt	Jell-O
Sesame seeds	Marmalade
Soups (canned):	Mixed dried fruit
asparagus, celery, etc.	Mixed spices
Sour cream	Nutmeg
Soy sauce	Puff pastry and short crust
Spaghetti and noodles	pastry
Vegetable broth	Sugar (confectioners',
Vinegar	granulated, superfine, brown)
Worcestershire sauce	Vanilla cake mix
	Vanilla extract

BREAKFASTS

Eat breakfast like a king, lunch like a prince,
and dinner like a pauper.

—Adelle Davis

Almond Bread Slices

MAKES 15 SLICES

Recipe from Cyndi O'Meara.

4 egg whites
½ cup sugar
1 cup all-purpose flour
1 cup sliced almonds

Preheat the oven to 350°F. Beat egg whites until stiff, then add sugar and beat for 1 minute. Stir in flour and almonds. Place mixture in a lined loaf pan and bake for 40 minutes. Remove loaf from oven but leave oven on. When cool enough to handle, thinly slice loaf and place slices on a baking sheet. Return to oven for 10 minutes, or until browned.

Bacon & Egg Muffin

SERVES 1

A recipe from Brett McCosker.

1 egg
1 slice bacon
1 English muffin
1 tablespoon barbecue sauce

In a small skillet, fry egg and bacon; drain on paper towels. Toast muffin in a toaster, spread with barbecue sauce, and top with bacon and egg.

OPTIONAL: Add a slice of cheese.

Bircher Muesli

SERVES 1

½ cup natural muesli

¼ cup orange juice

2 tablespoons plain yogurt

1 green apple, grated

Soak muesli in juice for 15 minutes. Mix in remaining ingredients and serve.

Broiled Apple, Banana & Ricotta Stack

SERVES 1

This is a charming breakfast. Your guests will be impressed!

1 apple, sliced

1 banana, sliced

2 tablespoons fresh ricotta cheese

1 tablespoon honey

Preheat the broiler. Broil apple for 3 minutes, or until soft. On a plate, layer apple and banana. Top with ricotta and drizzle with honey.

OPTIONAL: This is also delicious done with pear rather than apple, or a combination of both.

Broiled Grapefruit

SERVES 2

2 medium grapefruit (Ruby Red and Rio Red are sweeter varieties)

1 tablespoon honey

1 tablespoon brown sugar

6 ounces vanilla yogurt

Preheat the broiler. Halve each grapefruit and carefully loosen segments with a sharp knife. Combine honey and brown sugar. Place grapefruit in a small ovenproof dish and drizzle with honey-sugar mixture. Broil for 3 to 4 minutes, or until slightly browned. Serve with yogurt.

Broiled Pears with Yogurt

SERVES 2

2 pears, halved lengthwise and cored

¼ cup yogurt (flavor of your choice)

Preheat the broiler. Broil pears cut sides up for 3 minutes, or until soft. Top with yogurt.

Chestnut Topping

SERVES 2

A delicious topping for pancakes.

3 tablespoons butter

1 tablespoon brown sugar

4 to 5 ounces cooked, peeled chestnuts, finely chopped

Melt butter in a small skillet. Add brown sugar and stir until dissolved. Add chestnuts and sauté until barely browned.

Chili & Sugar-Baked Bacon

SERVES 4

2 tablespoons mild chili powder

¾ cup packed brown sugar

12 thick slices smoked bacon

Preheat the oven to 325°F. Line a baking sheet with parchment paper. Mix chili powder and brown sugar in a shallow bowl. Bury each piece of bacon in the mix and rub both sides to coat well. Place bacon on baking sheet and bake for 30 minutes without turning, until nice and crispy.

Citrus Pancakes

SERVES 4

Our children love these.

1 cup self-rising flour

1 egg

1 cup milk

Finely grated zest of
1 orange

Pop flour into a bowl with a pinch of salt. Gradually beat in egg and milk until thick and smooth. Add orange zest. Heat a nonstick skillet. Pour desired quantity into skillet, cook until bubbling on top, and then flip.

OPTIONAL: Serve with maple syrup, lemon juice and sugar, honey, or stewed fruits.

English Muffin with Strawberries

SERVES 1

This is a really lovely way to start the day!

1 English muffin

2 teaspoons cream cheese

6 strawberries, quartered

2 tablespoons maple syrup

Cut muffin in half and toast. Spread cream cheese on both halves, top with strawberries, and drizzle with maple syrup.

Fluffy Cheese Omelet

SERVES 2

3 eggs, separated

½ cup finely grated cheese

1 tablespoon butter

Preheat the broiler. Beat whites of eggs stiffly with pinch of salt. Lightly fold in yolks and 3 tablespoons cold water, then grated cheese. Melt butter in a skillet and when very hot pour in egg mixture. Cook until golden brown underneath. Brown top under the broiler, or turn with a spatula.

Ham, Eggs & Green Tomatoes

SERVES 6

M.a.g.n.i.f.i.c.e.n.t!

6 round slices ham

6 eggs

1 green tomato, finely chopped

1 cup grated cheese (your favorite)

Preheat the oven to 350°F. Grease 6 Texas (large) muffin tin cups and line them with ham. Beat eggs and season with salt and pepper. Pour into the ham-lined cups. Top with tomato and cheese. Bake for 20 minutes, or until set.

Healthy Breakfast on the Go

SERVES 4

A fantastic breakfast to take with you.

6 ounces fruit yogurt

1 egg

2 cups diced watermelon

2 cups diced other fruit (banana, strawberries, pineapple, apples)

Put all ingredients into a blender and puree.

Huevos Rancheros

SERVES 6

2 cans (14.5 ounces each) diced tomatoes with onions and garlic

2 red bell peppers, chopped

2 fresh red chile peppers, seeded and chopped

6 eggs

In a large skillet, heat tomatoes over medium heat. Add bell peppers and chiles and cook until tender. Reduce heat and simmer for 5 minutes. Season with salt and black pepper to taste. Use a spoon to make 6 small wells in the sauce, and carefully crack the eggs into each well. Cover and poach for 3 to 4 minutes.

OPTIONAL: Add smoked paprika and bay leaves for extra flavor. Serve with warmed tortillas.

Praline Toast

¼ cup (½ stick) butter, softened

¼ cup pecans, finely chopped

½ cup brown sugar

8 slices bread

Preheat the oven to 350°F. Mix together butter, pecans, and sugar. Spread on bread slices and bake on a baking sheet until brown and bubbling.

Scones

MAKES 12

A recipe from the kitchen wonder herself, Daphne Beutel. This doesn't get any easier!

4 cups self-rising flour

1¼ cups heavy cream

1 cup lemonade

Preheat the oven to 400°F. Line a baking sheet with parchment paper. Sift flour into a bowl, make a well, and pour in cream and lemonade. With a knife, mix to make a firm dough. Turn out onto a lightly floured surface and gently knead until combined. Press with your hands until about 1 inch thick, cut with a 3-inch round cookie cutter, place on baking sheet close together, and bake for 12 minutes, or until golden brown.

OPTIONAL: These freeze beautifully.

Turkey Bacon & Eggs

SERVES 2

2 tablespoons olive oil

4 to 6 slices turkey bacon (depending on your appetite)

1 tomato, thickly sliced

2 eggs, beaten

In a skillet, heat 1 tablespoon of oil. Add turkey bacon and tomato and cook to your liking. Transfer to plates. Heat remaining 1 tablespoon oil in the same skillet over medium heat. Pour in eggs and scramble to your liking. Add to bacon and tomato, and enjoy.

Waffles, Strawberries & Yogurt

SERVES 4

8 waffles, frozen or homemade

8 ounces strawberries, quartered

6 ounces vanilla yogurt

Lightly toast waffles. Fold half the strawberries into yogurt and spoon over waffles. Top with remaining strawberries.

Zucchini Fritters

SERVES 2

2 eggs

¼ red onion, grated

½ zucchini, grated

2 tablespoons grated carrot

Beat eggs and add remaining ingredients. Season to taste. Heat a small nonstick skillet over medium heat. Spoon two portions of mixture into the pan, leaving room for spreading. Cook for 2 minutes on each side.

APPETIZERS

Every person is a new door to a different world.

—From the film *Six Degrees of Separation*

Apricots & Blue Cheese

MAKES 12 HALVES

6 large fresh apricots

2 ounces mild blue cheese

12 walnuts, chopped

Halve and pit apricots and stuff with blue cheese and walnuts.

Asparagus Canapés

SERVES 6 TO 8

A recipe from Wendy Beattie. Like the lady, absolutely fabulous!

4 ounces sliced prosciutto

Half a 5-ounce wheel of Camembert cheese

2 bunches asparagus, trimmed

Preheat the oven to 300°F. With scissors, cut prosciutto into ½-inch strips. Cut the Camembert into long, thin strips. Lay prosciutto flat horizontally, and place 1 asparagus spear at right angles to the ham. Lay a slice of Camembert along the asparagus and roll the prosciutto around its contents. Place on a baking sheet and bake until the cheese has melted. Serve hot.

Baked Brie

SERVES 4

1 sheet puff pastry

1 wheel Brie cheese (about 1 pound)

1 tablespoon cranberry relish

1 egg, beaten

Preheat the oven to 350°F. Line a baking sheet with parchment paper. Roll pastry out to ⅛-inch thickness. Place Brie in center of pastry. Top with cranberry relish, then wrap pastry around cheese, sealing the edges by pressing with a fork or your finger. Place on baking sheet seam side down. Brush with the beaten egg. Bake for 15 to 20 minutes, until golden. Remove from the oven and let rest for 15 to 20 minutes before serving.

OPTIONAL: Serve with apple slices, toast rounds, crackers, or raw vegetables. And if you have them, sprinkle with poppy seeds prior to baking.

Brie Bruschetta

SERVES 6 TO 8

1 loaf crusty French bread, cut into 1-inch slices

2 large vine-ripened tomatoes, chopped (save juices)

1 wheel Brie cheese (about 8 ounces)

½ bunch fresh basil leaves

Preheat the broiler. Place bread on a baking sheet and broil to toast one side. Remove from broiler (but leave broiler on), turn slices over, and brush untoasted sides with some of the juices from the chopped tomatoes. Cut the Brie into slices that will fit on the toasted bread slices. Lay slices of Brie on the bread. Return to the broiler for 2 to 3 minutes, or until cheese is melted. Top with tomatoes and shredded basil leaves and season with sea salt and pepper.

Cheddar Pennies

MAKES 20

4 tablespoons butter (½ stick), softened

1 cup grated Cheddar cheese

⅓ cup all-purpose flour

⅛ to ¼ teaspoon chili powder

With an electric mixer, cream butter until soft. Stir in the remaining ingredients to form a dough. Transfer to a lightly floured surface. Shape into a cylinder about 1¼ inches in diameter. Wrap in wax paper and refrigerate for 1 to 2 hours. Preheat the oven to 350°F. Line a baking sheet with parchment paper. Slice the dough into ¼-inch-thick rounds and place on the sheets. Bake for 12 to 15 minutes, or until golden. Transfer to a rack to cool.

Cheese Pies

MAKES 16

These little melt-in-the-mouth pies are best eaten warm.

2 sheets puff pastry

8 ounces feta cheese

8 ounces mozzarella cheese, grated

2 eggs, lightly beaten (reserve a little for brushing the pastry)

Preheat the oven to 400°F. Line a baking sheet with parchment paper. With a 4-inch round cookie cutter, cut 16 rounds of puff pastry. (We used a cup as a cookie cutter.) Set aside. In a bowl, mash feta cheese with a fork. Mix in mozzarella and then add eggs. Put 1 tablespoon of the filling on one half of each round of pastry. Slightly dampen pastry edges, then fold over filling to make half-moons. Seal the pies by pressing down with the tines of a fork. Brush with reserved beaten egg for a presentable finish. Place on baking sheet and bake for 15 to 20 minutes, or until puffed and golden.

Chicken & Chorizo Skewers

MAKES 12

1 skinless, boneless chicken breast, cubed

1 chorizo sausage, sliced

Extra virgin olive oil spray

½ cup salsa

Thread meats onto skewers (or toothpicks, for bite-size servings). Spray lightly before grilling. Serve warm with salsa as a dipping sauce.

Chiles con Queso

SERVES 6

*This is just **soooo** very tasty. Serve on a large platter surrounded by corn chips or fresh vegetable sticks.*

1 can (14.5 ounces) diced tomatoes, drained, juice reserved

1 Spanish onion, diced

2 red chile peppers, seeded and diced

½ pound Cheddar cheese, grated

Preheat the oven to 350°F. In a microwaveable oven-safe dish, combine drained tomatoes, onion, chiles, and cheese (leaving a handful of cheese for topping later). Add just enough tomato juice to cover the ingredients. Season with salt and pepper to taste and microwave on high for 5 minutes. Remove, top with reserved cheese, and bake for 10 minutes, or until the cheese on top is golden and bubbling.

Crab Dip

MAKES 1½ CUPS

Recipe from Cyndi O'Meara.

8 ounces cream cheese, softened

¾ cup Thai sweet chili sauce

1 cup crabmeat

Spread cream cheese on a small platter. Cover with chili sauce and sprinkle with crabmeat.

Cucumber Wedges

SERVES 6 TO 8

2 medium cucumbers

1 tablespoon lime juice

1½ teaspoons chili powder

Cut cucumbers lengthwise into quarters and cut each quarter crosswise into 2-inch pieces. Place cucumbers in a single layer on a serving plate. Drizzle with lime juice. Sprinkle with chili powder and 1 teaspoon coarse salt.

OPTIONAL: Szechuan pepper instead of chili powder is a nice change.

Curried Eggs

MAKES 12 HALVES

An Australian barbecue classic.

6 hard-cooked eggs

2 tablespoons mayonnaise

½ teaspoon curry powder

1 teaspoon finely chopped parsley

Peel eggs and halve lengthwise. Remove yolks and mash. Add mayonnaise, curry powder, parsley, and sea salt and pepper to taste. Put yolk mixture back into the egg halves and chill before serving.

French Onion Dip

MAKES 1 CUP

2 tablespoons French onion
soup mix

1 cup sour cream

Mix soup into sour cream and chill.

Fried Camembert

SERVES 4

This is sooooo easy and a real crowd pleaser!

1 wheel Camembert cheese
(about 8 ounces), well
chilled

1 egg

¼ cup fine bread crumbs

1 cup rice bran oil

Cut Camembert into equal wedges.
Lightly beat egg. Dip each cheese
wedge into the beaten egg, turning
to coat, and then roll in bread crumbs.
Cover and refrigerate. Deep-fry in the
oil, turning regularly, until golden brown
in color.

OPTIONAL: Add ¼ cup of sesame seeds to bread crumbs for a little
crunch. Serve with cranberry sauce.

Fundido with Chorizo & Tortilla Chips
SERVES 4 TO 6

2 ounces fresh chorizo sausage, casings removed

2½ cups shredded mozzarella cheese (10 ounces)

2 scallions, thinly sliced

Tortilla chips, for serving

Preheat the broiler. In a skillet, cook chorizo over medium heat until nicely browned. Drain off the fat. Cover the bottom of a small broilerproof dish with mozzarella and broil until golden and bubbling. Remove and top with chorizo. Return to the broiler for 3 minutes to crisp chorizo. Remove and garnish with scallions. Serve immediately with tortilla chips.

Garlic & Cilantro Pita Crisps
SERVES 4

Yummy!

½ cup olive oil

1 tablespoon minced garlic

1 tablespoon finely chopped cilantro

1 large pita bread (7-inch diameter)

Preheat the oven to 375°F. Combine oil, garlic, and cilantro in a small bowl. Split pita bread in half to make 2 circles, and brush rough side of each circle with oil mixture. Cut each circle into 6 wedges. Place on a baking sheet and bake uncovered for 5 to 6 minutes, or until golden brown and crisp.

Garlic Avocado Dip

MAKES 1 CUP

2 avocados

2 large cloves garlic

½ lemon

Peel avocado, reserving pit. Place 1 teaspoon sea salt and garlic in a mortar and pound with a pestle until well combined. Place avocado and garlic paste in a food processor together with the juice of ½ lemon. Mix well and check seasoning. Put pit back into dip to help prevent discoloration. Refrigerate until needed.

Golden Cheese Puffs

MAKES 24

1 pound Cheddar cheese

6 eggs

2 teaspoons chili powder

½ cup peanut oil

Grate the cheese and melt it very gently in a heavy saucepan over low heat or in a double boiler over hot water. Separate the eggs, then beat the whites until stiff peaks form and set aside. Beat the yolks until smooth, then stir them into the cheese. Mix well and remove from the heat. Stir in the chili powder, fold in the egg whites, and combine well to make a batter. Heat 1 inch of oil in a skillet or a deep-fryer. Drop the batter by the spoonful into the hot oil and fry for 3 to 4 minutes, or until golden. Drain the puffs on paper towels and serve hot.

Grilled Cheese Salsa Dip

SERVES 4

A Mexicana marvel—too easy and too tasty!

8 ounces Edam or Gouda cheese, shredded

2 tablespoons cream

½ cup salsa

Place cheese in a small saucepan. Cook over medium-low heat until melted. Add cream, stirring frequently to make sure cheese doesn't scorch. Transfer to a warm dish and top with salsa.

OPTIONAL: Serve with fresh raw vegetables and corn chips.

Holy Guacamole

MAKES 1½ CUPS

3 avocados

½ cup salsa

¼ cup sour cream

Corn chips

Mash avocados. Add salsa, sour cream, and a pinch of sea salt and mix well. Serve with corn chips.

Honey & Orange Shrimp

SERVES 4

A recipe by Susan Smith.

1 orange

2 teaspoons olive oil

2 tablespoons honey

24 jumbo shrimp, peeled and deveined

Finely grate 1 tablespoon zest from orange. Squeeze and measure out 2 tablespoons juice. Combine oil, zest, juice, and honey in a bowl. Add shrimp, toss to coat, and marinate in the fridge for 1 hour. Cook in a hot nonstick skillet until shrimp have turned orange in color.

OPTIONAL: Serve with Soy-Ginger Dipping Sauce (page 50).

Hummus

MAKES ABOUT 1 CUP

A recipe by Michelle Dodd.

1 can (10.5 ounces) chickpeas, rinsed and drained

1 clove garlic, crushed

2 tablespoons lemon juice

1 tablespoon tahini

Blend all ingredients in a food processor.

OPTIONAL: Serve with crackers and julienned vegetables.

Kahlúa Dip

SERVES 8

Yummy!

1 cup sour cream

3 tablespoons brown sugar

¼ cup Kahlúa

Fresh seasonal fruit for dipping: strawberries, pineapple, apple, cantaloupe

Combine sour cream, sugar, and Kahlúa in a bowl, cover, and chill for 30 minutes before serving. Transfer to a serving bowl, place on a platter, and surround with fresh fruit to dip.

Lemon-Rosemary Baked Olives

SERVES 8

1 pound pitted green and black olives

Zest of 1 lemon

2 sprigs rosemary, leaves only

2 cloves garlic, thinly sliced

Preheat the oven to 400°F. Place olives in a baking dish and, with a rolling pin, gently push down so skin splits. Mix in the lemon zest, rosemary, and garlic. Bake for 15 minutes and serve warm.

OPTIONAL: Drizzle 1 tablespoon of olive oil over the olives before baking.

Minted Lamb Balls

SERVES 4

A recipe from Janelle McCosker.

1 pound ground lamb

2 teaspoons curry powder

Leaves of 6 sprigs mint, chopped

Mix all ingredients together and roll into bite-size balls. Fry in a nonstick skillet until crunchy on the outside (this means the meat is cooked well on the inside).

OPTIONAL: These are lovely served with raita as a dipping sauce.

Mozzarella Cubes

SERVES 4

8 ounces mozzarella cheese

2 eggs

1 cup Ritz cracker crumbs

¼ cup extra-virgin olive oil

Cut mozzarella into 1-inch cubes. Lightly beat the eggs. Dip the cheese cubes into the egg and then into the cracker crumbs. Heat the oil in a skillet. (The oil is ready when a 1-inch cube of bread sizzles immediately after being dropped into it.) Fry the cheese cubes until golden brown.

TIP: For best results, ensure mozzarella is cold and make cracker crumbs in a food processor.

Nachos with Chiles & Olives

SERVES 4

4 ounces tortilla chips

6 tablespoons sliced pickled jalapeño chiles

4 ounces black olives, pitted and sliced

4 ounces shredded Cheddar cheese

Preheat the oven to 350°F. Lay tortilla chips in a large ovenproof dish. Sprinkle with jalapeños, olives, and Cheddar and bake for 12 to 15 minutes, or until cheese is melted and bubbling.

Nin's Easy & Tasty Mushrooms

MAKES 12

"Nin" is Jan Neale, Kim's lovely mother-in-law.

12 medium mushrooms

Thai sweet chili sauce

4 ounces Brie cheese

Preheat the broiler. Wash and stem mushrooms and place on a baking sheet, stem side up. Place a dollop of sweet chili sauce in the middle of each mushroom and top with a sliver of Brie cheese. Broil until Brie melts.

OPTIONAL: Garnish with fresh herbs.

Oysters Champagne

MAKES 6

*Thanks, Spud, for this and
the following ever-popular oyster recipes!*

6 oysters on the half shell

¼ teaspoon minced fresh
ginger

⅓ cup Champagne

¼ teaspoon chopped mint

Place washed oysters on a serving
plate. Combine ginger, Champagne,
and mint and spoon over oysters. Serve
immediately.

Oysters Kilpatrick

MAKES 6

6 oysters on the half shell

1 slice bacon, finely diced

¼ cup barbecue sauce

¼ cup tomato sauce

Preheat the broiler. Place washed oysters
on a baking sheet. Combine bacon and
sauces. Spoon the mixture onto oysters
and broil until oysters begin to bubble
and bacon is crisp but not burned.

Oysters Mexicano

MAKES 6

6 oysters on the half shell

½ lime, juiced

6 corn chips

¼ cup guacamole

Place washed oysters on a serving plate
and pour lime juice evenly over them.
Spoon on guacamole and stud with a
corn chip for serving.

Paprika Dip

MAKES ¾ CUP

¾ cup crème fraîche

1 teaspoon smoked paprika

Mix crème fraîche and paprika and chill before serving.

OPTIONAL: Serve with your favorite crackers or fresh vegetable sticks.

Pear & Roquefort Bites

MAKES 12

2 pears, peeled and cut into 1-inch cubes

¼ pound Roquefort cheese, cut into 1-inch cubes

Thread one cube of each onto a toothpick and serve immediately.

Quesadilla

SERVES 4

Sensational served with a Corona and lime.

¼ cup tahini

4 flour tortillas

2 cups grated mozzarella cheese

4 teaspoons mixed herbs (fresh or dried)

Preheat the oven to 300°F. Smear tahini on flour tortillas and season with sea salt and pepper. Sprinkle on mozzarella and herbs. Fold each tortilla in half. Place on a baking sheet and bake for 10 to 12 minutes, or until golden. Cut into wedges to serve.

Ricotta & Chutney Dip

MAKES ABOUT 1½ CUPS

1 cup ricotta cheese

½ cup mango chutney (or any fruit chutney)

¼ cup mixed nuts, chopped

Pappadums

Mix ricotta and chutney until well combined, then stir in nuts. Serve with pappadums.

Salmon Pitas

SERVES 6

A timeless canapé from Kendra Horwood.

6 mini pita breads

7 ounces smoked salmon

6 ounces crème fraîche

Watercress

Top pitas with smoked salmon, a dollop of crème fraîche, and watercress to garnish.

OPTIONAL: Substitute fresh dill for the watercress.

Savory Scrolls

SERVES 6

A recipe from the beautiful Lisa Darr.

2 tablespoons tomato paste

1 sheet puff pastry, just thawed

2 slices bacon, chopped and lightly fried

¼ cup grated Parmesan cheese

Preheat the oven to 350°F. Spread tomato paste over the sheet of pastry. Scatter bacon and cheese over the tomato paste. Roll into a log. Cut crosswise into pinwheels (1 inch thick), place on a baking sheet, and bake for 15 minutes, or until pastry turns golden brown.

Smoked Salmon Dip

MAKES ABOUT 1 CUP

10 ounces smoked salmon, finely chopped

2 tablespoons cream

1 teaspoon horseradish sauce

1 teaspoon chopped chives

Combine all ingredients and mix well.

OPTIONAL: Pile onto thick slices of cucumber or pita.

Spanish Omelet

SERVES 4 TO 6

1 pound potatoes, peeled and thinly sliced

2 tablespoons olive oil

1 onion, grated

4 eggs

Season potatoes with sea salt. Heat oil in a large nonstick skillet and add potatoes. Stir until they are slightly browned. Add onion and cook for 3 to 4 minutes. Beat eggs and add to skillet. Cook until the underside is golden brown and then turn to brown the other side. Remove from heat and let cool for 2 minutes before cutting into wedges to serve.

Spinach & Ricotta Scrolls

MAKES 12

A recipe from Wendy Beattie. Excellent for entertaining!

1 package (10 ounces) frozen chopped spinach, thawed and squeezed dry

½ cup ricotta cheese

1 cup grated mozzarella or Cheddar cheese

3 sheets puff pastry

Preheat the oven to 350°F. Combine spinach, ricotta, and mozzarella cheese and mix well. Season with sea salt and pepper. Halve each pastry sheet lengthwise, then halve each piece on the diagonal so you have 12 long triangular strips. Place a heaping tablespoon of mixture at the widest end and roll to enclose. Place on a baking sheet and bake for 20 to 25 minutes, or until golden.

OPTIONAL: Baste with beaten egg before baking for a really presentable finish.

Spinach Bread Bowl

SERVES 6 TO 8

A fabulous recipe from Jocelyn Wilson.

1 bunch fresh spinach, chopped, or 1 box (10 ounces) frozen chopped spinach, thawed and excess liquid squeezed out

1½ cups sour cream

1 envelope spring vegetable soup mix

1 round loaf bread (about 1 pound)

In a large pot of boiling water, cook the spinach for 15 seconds to soften. Drain well, squeezing gently to remove excess liquid. In a bowl, combine sour cream, soup mix, and spinach and let sit for 15 minutes. Cut lid from the loaf of bread. Scoop out the middle of the loaf and cut into chunks. Pour the spinach mixture into the bread bowl and place on a baking sheet. Bake in a preheated 350°F oven for 20 minutes, or until warmed through and edges of the bread bowl turn golden brown. Add bread chunks for the final 5 to 6 minutes to toast. Use these as dippers when serving.

Strawberry Sweet & Sour

SERVES 4

A recipe from Lorraine Leeson. This will make an impact—TRY!!!

¼ cup brown sugar

½ cup sour cream

1 pound strawberries

Place brown sugar and sour cream in separate ramekins. To eat, dip a strawberry into sour cream and then into brown sugar.

Strawberry-Camembert Sticks

MAKES 6

½ cup balsamic vinegar

8 ounces strawberries

1 round Camembert cheese (4 to 5 ounces), cut into small wedges

Simmer vinegar in a small pan until reduced by half and syrupy. Let cool. Thread strawberries and Camembert onto skewers. Drizzle with balsamic syrup just before serving.

Tandoori Wings

SERVES 6

D.E.L.I.C.I.O.U.S!

⅓ cup tandoori paste

⅓ cup plain yogurt

1 medium onion, grated

2½ pounds chicken wings

Combine tandoori paste, yogurt, and onion in a large bowl. Add chicken and coat generously. Cover and refrigerate for at least 3 hours. Preheat the oven to 400°F. Place chicken in a large shallow baking dish (may need oil if nonstick). Roast, uncovered, for 30 minutes, or until chicken is well browned and cooked through.

Tangy Cheese Balls

SERVES 4

4 ounces cream cheese, softened

¼ cup finely crumbled blue cheese

2 tablespoons grated orange zest

⅓ cup mixed nuts, finely chopped

Combine cream cheese, blue cheese, and orange zest. Form into small balls and roll in nuts. Chill for 1 hour, or until firm, and serve.

SAUCES & SALSAS

Let food be your medicine and medicine be your food.

—Hippocrates

Avocado Salsa

A divinely delicious dip from Michelle Dodd.

1 avocado

½ vine-ripened tomato, diced

½ red onion, diced

3 tablespoons chopped cilantro

Dice avocado, reserving pit. Combine avocado, tomato, and onion. Add cilantro. Season with sea salt and pepper and mix. Place the pit back in the dip to help prevent discoloration. Refrigerate until needed.

OPTIONAL: Serve with a stack of fresh vegetable sticks.

Barbecue Stir-fry Sauce

MAKES ABOUT ½ CUP

Absolutely delicious in a beef stir-fry.

½ cup barbecue sauce

2 teaspoons minced fresh ginger

2 tablespoons soy sauce

Simply mix.

Best "In-a-Hurry" Sauce

MAKES ½ CUP

Serve with any meat and Asian steamed vegetables.

1 clove garlic, crushed

¼ cup Thai sweet chili sauce

¼ cup soy sauce

2 teaspoons grated fresh ginger

Combine all ingredients and mix well.

Caramel Sauce

MAKES 2 CUPS

This is heaven served over just about anything!

1 cup heavy cream

¾ cup brown sugar

¾ cup (1½ sticks) unsalted butter

Combine all ingredients in a small saucepan and bring to a boil over medium heat. Simmer, stirring gently, for 2 minutes, or until lovely and smooth.

Chili Mayonnaise

MAKES ABOUT ½ CUP

Delicious served with Sweet Potato Oven Fries (page 90).

½ teaspoon sambal oelek

⅓ cup mayonnaise

¼ teaspoon ground cumin

2 tablespoons sour cream

Combine all ingredients in a bowl and mix well.

OPTIONAL: Add 1 tablespoon chopped cilantro.

Cinnamon Sauce

MAKES ABOUT 1 CUP

Serve drizzled over baked apples, apple pie, and basic cheesecakes.

2 tablespoons butter

½ cup brown sugar

1 rounded teaspoon cinnamon

2 teaspoons cornstarch

In a small saucepan, combine butter, brown sugar, and cinnamon and bring to a boil over medium heat. Dissolve cornstarch in 2 tablespoons water; whisk into hot syrup for a smooth sauce. Cover and keep warm until serving.

Cocktail Sauce

MAKES 1 CUP

A delicious accompaniment to most seafood.

½ cup mayonnaise

½ cup ketchup

½ teaspoon Worcestershire sauce

2 tablespoons cream

Combine all ingredients in a bowl and stir well. Season with sea salt and pepper.

Corn Salsa

MAKES 2 CUPS

Sensational!

2 ears of corn, husked

1 red onion, finely diced

½ red bell pepper, finely chopped

1 tablespoon lemon juice

Cook corn in a small saucepan of salted boiling water for 5 minutes or until tender. Let cool slightly, then cut kernels from cob. Combine corn, onion, bell pepper, and lemon juice in a medium bowl. Taste and season with salt and pepper.

OPTIONAL: Toss in a little chopped fresh cilantro before serving.

Cranberry Relish

MAKES 1 CUP

Beautiful served with all kinds of grilled and roast poultry and as a dipping sauce on a cheese platter.

2 oranges

¾ cup packed brown sugar

2 teaspoons finely chopped fresh ginger

1 bag (12 ounces) fresh or frozen cranberries

Grate the zest from 1 orange. Set zest aside. Squeeze both oranges for juice. In a small saucepan, combine 2 teaspoons of the orange juice and all the brown sugar. Heat slowly and continue cooking until sugar begins to caramelize; be careful not to let it burn. Add the ginger and orange zest. Cook for 1 minute, then add the cranberries, remaining orange juice, and ½ teaspoon pepper. Cook over medium-high heat, stirring frequently for 5 minutes, or until the cranberries are slightly broken but not mushy (frozen cranberries will take about 7 minutes). Remove from the heat and let cool.

Easy Mocha Sauce

MAKES ABOUT 2 CUPS

Delicious served with Quick Poached Pears (page 204).

1 cup chopped dark chocolate

1¼ cups heavy cream

2 teaspoons instant coffee granules

Combine all ingredients and cook in the microwave for 2 minutes, stopping to stir halfway.

Easy Satay

MAKES 1 CUP

½ cup chunky peanut butter

2 tablespoons Thai sweet chili sauce

¾ cup vegetable broth

1 tablespoon chopped cilantro

Combine peanut butter, sweet chili sauce, and broth in a small saucepan. Cook, stirring constantly, for 2 to 3 minutes. Serve topped with cilantro.

OPTIONAL: Delicious served with vegetable crudités: cucumber, carrot, celery, cherry tomatoes, etc.

Garlic Butter

MAKES ¼ CUP

¼ cup (½ stick) butter, softened

2 cloves garlic, crushed

1 teaspoon lemon juice

1 tablespoon finely chopped parsley

Mix all together and season with sea salt and pepper.

OPTIONAL: Make slices in a loaf of French bread an inch apart. Spread the garlic butter generously in the slices. Cover with foil and bake in a 325° to 350°F oven for 10 minutes.

Gremolata

MAKES ABOUT ¼ CUP

*Gremolata acts as a palate cleanser and
is lovely as a garnish on grilled or roasted lamb,
pork chops, beef, and even roasted potatoes.*

Grated zest of 1 lemon

1 clove garlic, crushed

2 tablespoons finely
chopped parsley

1 teaspoon olive oil

Thoroughly combine all ingredients in a small bowl with ½ teaspoon salt and ¼ teaspoon black pepper. Cover with plastic wrap. Refrigerate for 1 hour before serving.

Grilled Corn & Zucchini Salsa

SERVES 6

2 ears of corn, unhusked

¼ pound baby zucchini,
halved lengthwise

2 avocados, coarsely
chopped

2 tablespoons bottled lime
vinaigrette

Cook corn (in the husk) and zucchini on an outdoor grill or stovetop grill pan until tender. When cool enough to handle, chop zucchini. Remove the corn husks and use a sharp knife to remove kernels from the cobs. Combine corn, zucchini, and avocado. Drizzle with dressing and toss gently to mix.

OPTIONAL: Add some halved grape tomatoes if you have them. This is divine served on top of grilled chicken, fish, or pork. Also delicious if you make your own Lime & Chili Dressing (page 74).

Honey-Soy Garlic Marinade

MAKES 1 CUP

This is lovely on poultry and pork, especially ribs.

10 tablespoons honey

Juice of 1 lemon

6 tablespoons soy sauce

4 cloves garlic, crushed

Mix all ingredients together, smear onto meat, and allow to marinate for at least 2 hours before grilling.

Horseradish Cream

MAKES ½ CUP

This is incredible served with roast beef and corned beef.

½ cup sour cream

2 tablespoons horseradish sauce

2 teaspoons chopped scallions

1 teaspoon white balsamic or white wine vinegar

Combine sour cream, horseradish sauce, scallions, and vinegar in a small bowl. Refrigerate until ready to serve.

Horseradish, Mustard & Walnut Cream Sauce

MAKES 1 CUP

Lovely served with fish or chicken.

¾ cup sour cream

1 tablespoon Dijon mustard

¼ cup horseradish sauce

½ cup walnuts, toasted and finely chopped

Mix all ingredients well.

Mango Salsa

MAKES 1 CUP

Delectable served with grilled chicken or seafood.

Grated zest and juice of ½ lime

½ jalapeño pepper, seeded and finely chopped

1 cup mango cubes

3 sprigs cilantro, finely chopped

Combine all ingredients and add sea salt and black pepper to taste.

Mixed Berry Sauce

MAKES 1 CUP

Spoon over vanilla ice cream or cheesecake. . . . Scrummy!

½ cup heavy cream

¼ cup packed brown sugar

1 cup frozen mixed berries

In a small saucepan, heat cream and sugar, stirring until sugar dissolves. Add mixed berries and cook, stirring, for 2 minutes. Let cool before serving.

Onion Jam

MAKES 1 CUP

This is a great topper on steak.

3 large Spanish onions, slivered

2 tablespoons extra virgin olive oil

3 tablespoons balsamic vinegar

½ cup packed brown sugar

Add onion to a preheated pot with the oil and cook until completely collapsed. Stir in vinegar and sugar, reduce heat to low, and simmer, stirring occasionally, until the mixture has a jamlike consistency.

Parmesan Butter

*Serve with steak, lamb, or chicken or
on a warm fresh baguette.*

½ cup (1 stick) butter, softened

¼ cup grated Parmesan cheese

2 cloves garlic, crushed

1 tablespoon minced fresh basil

Combine all ingredients in a small bowl.

Pesto Pleasure

MAKES ¾ CUP

*Serve with pasta, potatoes, or steamed
green vegetables such as asparagus or broccoli.*

½ cup sour cream

¼ cup pesto, e.g., basil

Mix together.

Soy-Ginger Dipping Sauce

MAKES ⅓ CUP

This is d.e.l.i.c.i.o.u.s served with
Honey & Orange Shrimp (page 25).

⅓ cup soy sauce

2 teaspoons sugar

½- to ¾-inch piece of ginger, grated

Combine all ingredients in a small saucepan. Stir over low heat until sugar dissolves.

White Sauce

MAKES 1 CUP

2 tablespoons butter

2 tablespoons flour

1 cup milk

Melt butter in a saucepan and remove from heat. Stir in flour and blend in milk. Return to heat, stir until sauce boils and thickens, and simmer for 2 minutes. Season with sea salt and pepper and add extra milk if required.

Yogurt Dipping Sauce

MAKES 1 CUP

A lovely healthy accompaniment to any Indian-spiced dish.

¾ cup plain yogurt

1 medium cucumber, finely diced

2 tablespoons lemon juice

1 tablespoon chopped mint leaves

Combine all ingredients in a serving bowl.

LIGHT LUNCHES

After thirty, a body has a mind of its own.

—Bette Midler

Antipasto Tarts

MAKES 12

Scrumptious!

2 sheets puff pastry

8 ounces antipasto mix (see Tip)

3 eggs

1⅓ cups sour cream

Preheat the oven to 350°F. Using a 3½-inch round cookie cutter, cut 12 rounds out of puff pastry sheets. Line the cups of a nonstick muffin tin with the pastry rounds. Divide antipasto mix among the cups. Lightly whisk eggs, add sour cream, and season with sea salt and pepper. Pour over tarts and bake for 20 minutes.

OPTIONAL: Add a splash of ketchup and Worcestershire sauce to the egg mix. Top with a sprinkle of Parmesan cheese before baking.

TIP: If your market doesn't have an olive bar with premixed antipasto, just buy a selection of sun-dried tomatoes, feta, and olives for a total of 8 ounces.

Asparagus Soup

SERVES 4

1 can (15 ounces) asparagus, drained (liquid reserved)

1 can (10.75 ounces) condensed cream of chicken soup

½ teaspoon minced fresh ginger

Toasted bread fingers

In a saucepan, combine asparagus and liquid from the can. Add soup, 1 cup water, and ginger. Season with pepper. Bring to a simmer and cook for 10 minutes. Transfer to a blender and puree until smooth. Serve with bread fingers.

Bacon Pizza

SERVES 1

A recipe from the delightful Veronica Griffin.

3 slices bacon

3 tablespoons pizza sauce

1 pita

¼ cup shredded mozzarella cheese

Preheat the broiler. Dice bacon and fry for 2 minutes. Spread pizza sauce on pita bread, sprinkle with bacon, and top with mozzarella cheese. Place pizza directly on oven rack or on a pizza pan and broil until the cheese browns and bubbles.

Baked Potato with Chili con Carne

SERVES 4

4 large baking potatoes

1 can (15 ounces) chili con carne, warmed

¼ cup sour cream

1 tablespoon chopped fresh chives

Preheat the oven to 350°F. Pierce potatoes with a knife several times, then wrap in foil. Bake for 40 minutes, or until soft. Remove from the oven, let stand for 5 minutes, remove foil, and cut a crisscross into each potato halfway through. Top with chili, a dollop of sour cream, and chives.

Baked Potato with Tomato Salsa

SERVES 1

1 baking potato (8 ounces)

¼ cup cottage cheese

2 tablespoons tomato salsa

1 tablespoon chopped fresh chives

Preheat the oven to 350°F. Pierce the potato with a knife several times, then wrap in foil. Bake for 40 minutes, or until soft. Remove from the oven, let stand for 5 minutes, remove foil, and cut a crisscross into the potato halfway through. Top with cottage cheese and salsa, and sprinkle with chives.

Basic Clam Chowder

SERVES 4

So easy, yet sooo tasty!

1 onion

3 potatoes, peeled and diced

1 quart steamed clams

2 cups milk

In a saucepan, cook onion in 2 tablespoons water until tender. Add potatoes and just enough water to cover them. Bring to a boil, reduce the heat, and simmer for 10 minutes, or until tender. Season with salt and pepper, then add the clam meat with juice. Just before serving, add milk and heat but do not boil.

OPTIONAL: Garnish with a sprinkle of parsley on top. Can substitute a can of smoked oysters for clams. . . . *Yummy!*

Basil Polenta

SERVES 4

A recipe from Spud, a chef.

1 cup polenta

2 tablespoons butter

¼ cup grated Parmesan cheese

¼ cup chopped basil

In a saucepan, bring 4 cups water to a boil. Sprinkle in polenta in a steady stream and cook, stirring, until mixture becomes thick, 10 to 15 minutes. Once all polenta is in, reduce the heat to low, add butter and Parmesan, and stir gently for 3 minutes longer. Fold in basil, season well, and serve.

OPTIONAL: Serve immediately. Yummy topped with sautéed onions, peppers, and a can of black beans.

Beef Koftas

MAKES 4 TO 6

½ cup chunky peanut butter

2 teaspoons curry powder

1 egg

1 pound lean ground beef

Warm peanut butter in the microwave on high for 30 seconds to soften. Mix in curry powder and egg. Add to ground beef and combine. Roll mixture into fat sausage shapes using ½ cup of mixture for each kofta. Broil or grill until cooked.

OPTIONAL: Serve as a burger or on pita bread with satay sauce and salad or separately as a patty with vegetables. *Yummmmm!*

Carrot & Cilantro Soup

SERVES 6

This soup sent the phone lines at QVC UK into meltdown!

8 cups vegetable broth

1 bunch cilantro, roots included, coarsely chopped

2 cloves garlic, crushed

6 carrots, coarsely chopped

In a medium saucepan, heat vegetable broth to warm. Add cilantro, garlic, and carrots. Bring to a boil, reduce to a simmer, and cook until carrots are tender. Season with sea salt and pepper. Transfer to a blender or food processor and puree.

OPTIONAL: Before serving, swirl in some sour cream.

Chantilly Soup

SERVES 4 TO 6

D.E.L.I.S.H.

4 cups fresh or frozen baby green peas

½ cup chopped parsley

2 scallions, chopped

6 cups vegetable broth

In a large saucepan, combine all the ingredients and bring to a boil. Reduce the heat and simmer for 10 minutes, or until the vegetables are quite tender. Remove from the heat and let cool before pureeing in a blender.

Cheese & Garlic Stack

SERVES 2

A recipe from Spud.

16 cloves garlic, peeled

3 flour tortillas (7-inch diameter)

1 cup grated Parmesan cheese

1 cup grated mozzarella cheese

Preheat the oven to 450°F. Wrap garlic in foil and roast in the oven for 15 minutes. Remove and let cool. (Leave the oven on.) Lay one tortilla on a baking sheet. Spread with one-third of the garlic, one-third of the Parmesan, and one-third of the mozzarella. Repeat layering with remaining ingredients. Bake for 15 minutes, or until the cheese bubbles and turns golden brown. Slice into wedges to serve.

Chili Dogs

MAKES 4

4 hot dogs, split lengthwise

1 can (10 ounces) condensed beef broth

1 can (14 ounces) chili con carne

4 hot dog rolls, split and toasted

In a skillet, brown hot dogs. Add broth and ¼ cup water, and cook over medium heat, stirring occasionally, for 8 minutes. In a separate saucepan, heat the chili con carne. Place drained hot dogs in toasted rolls and spoon the chili on top.

OPTIONAL: Top these with whatever extras your family likes. Recommendations we have had via Facebook are onions, grated cheese, sliced stuffed olives, jalapeños, chopped green pepper, and sliced pickles.

Derby Chicken Salad

SERVES 4

We love this American classic.

12 ounces skinless, boneless chicken breasts, cooked and cubed

4 ounces bacon, coarsely chopped and cooked until crisp

2 avocados, diced

16 cherry tomatoes, halved

Toss all ingredients together in a serving bowl and season with cracked black pepper to taste.

OPTIONAL: Drizzle with your favorite Italian salad dressing.

Easy Quesadilla

SERVES 4 HUNGRY PEOPLE!

½ cup sour cream

½ package taco seasoning

8 large flour tortillas

1 cup grated cheese (your favorite)

Mix together sour cream and taco seasoning. Spread 4 tortillas evenly with the sauce, then sprinkle with cheese. Top with remaining tortillas and then cook quesadillas one by one in a hot skillet. Flip after a minute or so, or whenever the bottom turns brown.

OPTIONAL: Add whatever fillings your lovely family will eat: jalapeños, olives, cooked onions, peppers, chicken, or ground beef.

French Onion Soup

SERVES 2

2 large onions, coarsely chopped

2 zucchini, coarsely chopped

1 envelope French onion soup mix

½ cup cream

Combine onions, zucchini, and soup mix in a saucepan with 4 cups water. Season with pepper and bring to a boil. Reduce to a simmer and cook for 30 minutes, stirring occasionally. Transfer to a blender or food processor and puree. Add cream, stir, and serve hot.

OPTIONAL: Top 2 thick slices of French bread with Gruyère and broil until melted. Place a cheese toast in the middle of the soup before serving.

Gourmet Pizza

SERVES 1

A recipe from Karyn Turnbull.

3 tablespoons peach chutney

1 pita

3 slices prosciutto, torn into strips

3 bocconcini, torn into strips

Preheat the oven to 350°F. Spread peach chutney over pita. Top with prosciutto and bocconcini. Place on a pizza pan or directly on the oven rack, and bake for 10 to 15 minutes.

Healthy Hamburgers

SERVES 4

4 beef patties (5 ounces each)

4 rye bread rolls

3 ounces grated Cheddar cheese

4 lettuce leaves

Broil or grill burgers. Cut rolls in half. Sprinkle cheese on bottom half of rolls. Top with burgers and lettuce.

OPTIONAL: Serve drizzled with your favorite sauce or ketchup.

Healthy Hot Dogs

SERVES 4

4 chicken sausages (about 4 ounces each)

4 wraps

3 ounces shredded cheese of your choice

1 cup shredded carrot, diced tomato, or sautéed onion

Broil or grill sausages. Sprinkle wraps with cheese and vegetable of choice. Add sausages, roll up, and serve.

OPTIONAL: Serve with ketchup or barbecue sauce. *Scrummy!*

Kabocha Soup

SERVES 4

Another simple main for a quick and easy lunch.

3 pounds kabocha squash, peeled and thinly sliced

1 large onion, chopped

5 chicken bouillon cubes

½ cup cream

In a large saucepan, combine squash, onion, bouillon cubes, and enough water to cover. Bring to a boil, reduce to a simmer, and cook for 20 minutes, or until tender. In batches, transfer mixture to a blender and puree. Return to the saucepan. Stir in cream and season with pepper. Cook until heated through.

OPTIONAL: Add ¼ teaspoon ground nutmeg and serve with fresh crusty bread.

Pea & Ham Soup

SERVES 4

3 cups chicken broth

3 cups frozen peas

5 fresh sage leaves

1 ham steak (8 ounces), finely chopped

In a saucepan, bring broth to a boil. Add peas and sage and cook for 5 minutes. Transfer to a blender or food processor and process until smooth. Return to the saucepan. Mix ham into soup and bring to a boil. Serve hot.

OPTIONAL: Accompany with crusty bread.

Popcorn Chicken

SERVES 4

1½ cups basmati rice

1½ pounds skinless, boneless chicken breasts

½ cup olive oil

1 to 2 tablespoons Cajun seasoning

Cook rice according to package directions. Meanwhile, pound chicken lightly and cut into small pieces. In a nonstick skillet, heat oil, add chicken, and stir-fry over medium heat. Before chicken has whitened, sprinkle on Cajun seasoning to taste. Keep cooking until well done and crispy black (looks burned but tastes yummy). Serve with rice.

Salmon & Asparagus Soup

SERVES 6

A recipe from Alexis Wallis.
Amazingly delicious for so little effort!

2 cans (5 ounces each) red salmon

1 can (10.75 ounces) condensed cream of asparagus soup

1¼ cups cream

Drain salmon, removing skin and bones, before pureeing in a blender. In a saucepan, mix blended salmon with cream of asparagus soup and 1 cup water. Add cream and bring to a bare simmer; do not boil. Season with pepper to taste.

Salt & Pepper Calamari

SERVES 6

Y.U.M.M.Y!

1 teaspoon Szechuan peppercorns

1 cup cornstarch

¾ pound calamari

1 cup sunflower oil

In a dry skillet, roast peppercorns until fragrant and beginning to crackle. Transfer to a mortar along with 1 teaspoon sea salt and grind. In a shallow bowl, combine pepper mixture and cornstarch. Roll calamari in the mixture, shaking off any excess. Deep-fry in hot oil in a hot wok for 1 minute, or until cooked. Drain and serve immediately.

Sweet Chili Chicken Wrap

SERVES 1

1 skinless, boneless chicken thigh, cut into chunks

1 tablespoon Thai sweet chili sauce

2 teaspoons soy sauce

1 sandwich wrap

Cook chicken in a heated nonstick skillet with sweet chili sauce and soy sauce until chicken is cooked, 5 to 10 minutes. Heat the wrap under a broiler for 1 to 2 minutes. Once warm, place the cooked chicken on the wrap and roll.

OPTIONAL: Add cilantro to chili and soy sauce mix.

Sweet Guacamole Wrap

SERVES 4 TO 6

You will be pleasantly surprised!

1 sweet potato

2 ripe avocados

8 whole wheat sandwich wraps

1 cup grated Cheddar cheese

Peel and thinly slice sweet potato. Gently steam until soft throughout, then remove from heat. Spoon out avocado flesh into a small bowl and mash with a fork. Lay each wrap flat and spread 1 tablespoon of avocado onto the surface, leaving a 1-inch border around the edges. Place 3 slices of the still warm sweet potato evenly on the avocado surface. Sprinkle 2 tablespoons of grated cheese onto the sweet potato. Roll wraps into logs and serve.

Thai Butternut Soup

SERVES 4

A recipe from Spud. THAI-RRIFIC!!

2¼ pounds butternut squash, peeled and diced

2 tablespoons red curry paste

1¼ cups coconut cream

¼ cup chopped cilantro

Sauté squash and red curry paste until the mixture starts to catch on the saucepan. Add coconut cream to deglaze the pan, top with enough water to be level with the squash, and bring to a boil. Reduce the heat and simmer until the squash becomes soft and mushy. Puree, season with sea salt and pepper, and fold in chopped cilantro.

Zucchini Soup

SERVES 2

A recipe from Jen Whittington.

2 zucchini, chopped

1 onion, coarsely chopped

1 envelope chicken soup mix

In a medium saucepan, place zucchini, onion, and soup mix with water to cover. Bring to a boil, then simmer for 30 minutes. Transfer to a blender in batches and puree until smooth. Season to taste and serve.

SIDES

What you focus on most you attract, so make each thought count toward your betterment rather than your detriment.

—Rachael Bermingham

All-American Coleslaw

SERVES 4 TO 6

1½ pounds green cabbage, quartered, cored, and shredded

3 tablespoons cider or malt vinegar

2 medium carrots

⅔ cup mayonnaise

In a large bowl, toss cabbage with vinegar and ¼ teaspoon salt. Grate carrots directly into the bowl. Add mayonnaise and toss well. Cover and refrigerate before serving.

Balsamic & Garlic Dressing

MAKES 1 CUP

2 tablespoons balsamic vinegar

¼ cup lemon juice

1 clove garlic, crushed

¾ cup olive oil

Combine all ingredients in a screw-top jar and shake well.

Balsamic-Chive Vinaigrette

MAKES 1 CUP

⅓ cup balsamic vinegar

1 tablespoon finely chopped chives

⅔ cup extra virgin olive oil

2 teaspoons superfine sugar

Combine dressing ingredients in a screw-top jar, adding 1 tablespoon of water and salt and pepper to taste. Shake really, really well. Taste and adjust seasonings, if required.

Basil & Lentil Salad

SERVES 4

Recipe from Shea Moor. 'Tis grand!

2 bunches fresh basil

1 can (14 ounces) brown lentils, drained

8 ounces cherry tomatoes, halved

½ Spanish onion, thinly sliced

Tear basil leaves from stems and place in a salad bowl. Add remaining ingredients and toss to combine.

OPTIONAL: This salad is delicious served drizzled with Classic Salad Dressing (page 73).

Blue Cheese Dressing

SERVES 8

Serve with Buffalo Wings (page 123) . . . Yummo!

¾ cup sour cream

1¼ cups mayonnaise

½ teaspoon dry mustard

4 ounces blue cheese, crumbled

In a large bowl, whisk together sour cream, mayonnaise, and mustard. Season with salt and pepper. Stir in blue cheese. Cover and refrigerate before serving; the longer you leave it, the longer the flavors have to develop.

Buttermilk Ranch Dressing

MAKES 2 CUPS

1 cup buttermilk

½ cup sour cream

½ cup mayonnaise

½ to 1 tablespoon garlic powder

Blend all ingredients together with salt and pepper to taste. Chill for at least 1 hour before serving.

OPTIONAL: Add 1 teaspoon onion powder.

Caesar Salad

SERVES 4

2 heads romaine lettuce, outer leaves discarded, leaves separated, rinsed, and dried

4 slices bacon, diced and cooked until crisp

3 ounces Parmesan cheese, shaved

Bottled Caesar salad dressing

Arrange lettuce in a large serving bowl. Scatter with bacon and Parmesan. Drizzle with Caesar dressing. Season with freshly ground black pepper.

OPTIONAL: Serve with quartered hard-cooked eggs.

Citrus Salad Dressing

MAKES ½ CUP

½ cup mayonnaise

3 tablespoons fresh orange juice

1 teaspoon nutmeg

Mix all ingredients together and season with pepper. Chill before serving over a green, leafy salad.

Classic Salad Dressing

MAKES ¾ CUP

½ cup lemon juice

¼ cup extra virgin olive oil

2 teaspoons Dijon mustard

2 cloves garlic, crushed

Place all ingredients in a screw-top jar, season with sea salt and pepper, and shake well.

OPTIONAL: This is divine served over the Basil & Lentil Salad (page 70).

Creamy Salad Dressing

MAKES 1 CUP

This is absolutely SENSATIONAL.
It will make a salad eater of anyone!!!

⅔ cup plain Greek yogurt

⅓ cup mayonnaise

Mix well, season, and serve over your favorite salad.

Easy Thai Dressing

MAKES ABOUT ½ CUP

2 tablespoons sugar

2 tablespoons lime juice

⅓ cup fish sauce

Chili powder, to taste

Combine all ingredients in a screw-top jar and shake well.

Honey Mustard Dressing
MAKES ABOUT ⅔ CUP

2 teaspoons honey

1½ tablespoons Dijon mustard

2 tablespoons white wine vinegar

½ cup extra virgin olive oil

Mix honey and mustard in a small bowl. Season with sea salt and pepper. Add vinegar and stir with a fork until completely dissolved. Slowly pour in oil while whisking vigorously. Taste and adjust seasonings, if necessary.

Lime & Chili Dressing
MAKES 1 CUP

¼ cup finely diced red onion

¼ cup coarsely chopped cilantro

1 tablespoon Thai sweet chili sauce

⅓ cup lime juice and ½ teaspoon grated lime zest

Mix all ingredients together and pour over salad or salsas.

Mango, Avocado & Bacon Salad

SERVES 4

This is a KNOCKOUT!!

2 large mangoes, cubed

2 avocados, cubed

8 slices bacon, cooked until crisp

Combine mango and avocado cubes in a salad bowl. Crumble in bacon and toss gently.

Mexican Coleslaw

SERVES 4 TO 6

Super tasty!

¼ red cabbage, shredded

1 carrot, grated

½ cup plain yogurt

½ teaspoon ground cumin

Combine all ingredients in a bowl and season with ⅛ teaspoon salt and 1 pinch freshly ground pepper. Serve at once or refrigerate and serve cold.

Mushroom Salad

SERVES 4

8 ounces mushrooms, thinly sliced

Grated zest and juice of ½ lemon

3 tablespoons crème fraîche

1 to 2 tablespoons chopped fresh chervil

Pop mushrooms into a bowl, sprinkle with lemon zest and juice, and season to taste with salt and pepper. Add crème fraîche and gently toss. Cover with plastic wrap and let stand, stirring once or twice, for 1 hour. Spoon into a serving bowl, sprinkle with chervil, and serve.

TIP: Chervil is a feathery green herb that tastes like a subtle blend of parsley and anise.

Orange & Almond Salad

SERVES 4

4 slices bacon, cooked until crisp and crumbled

½ head iceberg lettuce, shredded

2 oranges, peeled and sliced

⅓ cup slivered almonds, toasted

Combine all ingredients in a salad bowl. Refrigerate until ready to serve.

OPTIONAL: Dress with a balsamic vinaigrette.

Oranges & Cinnamon

SERVES 4

A delightful summer barbecue salad.

4 large oranges, chilled

½ teaspoon cinnamon

2 tablespoons shredded coconut, toasted

Peel oranges and thinly slice. Arrange the slices on crushed ice on a serving plate. Just before serving, sprinkle with cinnamon and coconut.

Potato Salad Dressing

MAKES 1 CUP

A recipe from the very talented Verna Day.

4 ounces cream cheese

⅔ cup sour cream

1 tablespoon chopped mint

1 tablespoon Thai sweet chili sauce

Combine all ingredients with an electric mixer and pour over cooked potatoes.

Red Salad

*This recipe from Perditta O'Connor
is a fabulous addition to any barbecue!*

1 pound watermelon (rind removed), sliced

½ Spanish onion, thinly sliced

2 to 3 tablespoons balsamic vinegar

Layer watermelon and onion in a serving dish and drizzle with balsamic vinegar.

Salmon & Caper Salad

SERVES 4

Kim's favorite.

1 can (4 ounces) salmon, drained

⅓ cup crumbled feta cheese

7 ounces baby arugula (or other salad greens)

1 tablespoon drained capers, chopped

Simply mix and enjoy!

Shrimp & Avocado Salad

SERVES 2

4 ounces mixed lettuces

1 large avocado, sliced

½ pound cooked shrimp, peeled and deveined

2 tablespoons Thousand Island dressing

Arrange lettuce, avocado, and shrimp on 2 plates. Drizzle with dressing.

OPTIONAL: Add 1 mango, cubed, and 1½ ounces macadamia nuts, lightly toasted and chopped, for a natural sweetness and crunch.

Tomato & Feta Salad

SERVES 4

A classic.

2 pounds tomatoes, thickly sliced

8 ounces feta cheese

½ cup extra virgin olive oil

16 kalamata olives, pitted

Arrange tomato slices on a serving plate. Crumble feta on top. Drizzle with olive oil and top with olives. Season to taste with sea salt and pepper. Cover and refrigerate for 30 minutes before serving.

Vinaigrette

MAKES 1¼ CUPS

½ cup olive oil

½ cup white wine vinegar

¼ cup finely chopped flat-
leaf parsley

2 teaspoons Dijon mustard

Combine all ingredients in a screw-top jar and shake well.

Waldorf Salad

SERVES 4

4 cups diced apples

¾ cup raisins

½ cup chopped pecans

½ cup mayonnaise

In a bowl, combine ingredients and refrigerate until ready to serve.

Wasabi Dressing

MAKES ⅔ CUP

A recipe by the dynamic Tanya Ormsby.

2 teaspoons wasabi paste

⅓ cup lemon juice

⅓ cup peanut oil

2 teaspoons finely chopped
fresh dill

Combine all ingredients in a screw-top jar and shake well.

POTATOES & RICE

Francisco Pizarro found the potato in Ecuador and brought it to Spain in the early sixteenth century. Thanks, Francisco!

Baked Rice

SERVES 4

2 tablespoons butter, melted

1 cup rice

2 cups beef broth

⅓ cup shredded Parmesan cheese

Preheat the oven to 350°F. Place butter in a baking dish, add rice, and pour beef broth over rice. Sprinkle with Parmesan and bake for 45 minutes.

Boiled Brown Rice

SERVES 4 TO 6

2 cups water

1 cup medium-grain brown rice

Bring water and rice to a boil, stirring occasionally. Reduce the heat, cover, and simmer for 15 to 20 minutes. Remove from heat and let stand, covered, for 5 minutes.

OPTIONAL: Buy the microwaveable bags of rice from the supermarket . . . even easier!

Coconut Rice

SERVES 4

1½ cups basmati rice

2 cans (14 ounces each) coconut milk

⅔ cup golden raisins

Good pinch of turmeric

In a large saucepan, combine rice, coconut milk, and 2 cups water and bring to a boil over high heat. Reduce the heat, add raisins, cover, and simmer over low heat for 25 minutes, or until liquid is absorbed and rice is tender. Stir often. Add turmeric for color and salt to taste.

Dirty Rice

SERVES 4

1 cup rice

1 tablespoon butter, softened

1 can (10.5 ounces) condensed onion soup

1 can (10.5 ounces) condensed beef consommé

Preheat the oven to 350°F. In a baking dish, mix all ingredients together with 1 cup water. Cover and bake for 40 minutes, or until the rice is nice and tender.

Easy Fried Rice

SERVES 4

S.C.R.U.M.P.T.I.O.U.S!

1 cup brown rice

2 slices bacon, diced

1 egg

¼ cup soy sauce

Cook rice according to package directions. Meanwhile, in a skillet, fry bacon until crisp. Pour off all but a skim of bacon fat. Crack the egg into the skillet, breaking the yolk to ensure spreading. Rinse rice under hot water, stirring it to separate. Drain thoroughly, add to bacon and egg, cover evenly with soy sauce, and toss well to heat through.

OPTIONAL: Also nice with diced red pepper, pineapple, peas, chopped scallion, or corn and a teaspoon or two of Thai sweet chili sauce.

Fluffy Rice Without a Cooker

SERVES 4 TO 6

Recipe from Cyndi O'Meara.

2½ cups long-grain white rice, washed

5 cups boiling water

Preheat the oven to 375°F. Place rice in a large glass baking dish with a lid. Add boiling water and stir until lump free. Cover and bake for 30 minutes.

Garlic Potatoes

SERVES 4

4 large potatoes, peeled and cut into ⅓-inch slices

1½ cups shredded mozzarella cheese

2 cloves garlic, crushed

1 cup sour cream

Preheat the oven to 350°F. Lightly steam potatoes for 15 minutes, or until just soft. Set aside. Combine 1 cup of the cheese, the garlic, and sour cream in a bowl and season. Cover the bottom of a baking dish with potatoes. Top with some of the sour cream mixture. Continue layering, ending with sour cream mixture. Top with remaining ½ cup cheese. Bake for 30 to 40 minutes, or until potatoes are soft.

Healthy Baked Potatoes

MAKES 4

4 small baking potatoes (about 5 ounces each)

½ cup Greek yogurt

1 tablespoon chopped parsley

1 tablespoon chopped chives

Preheat the oven to 450°F. Pierce each potato with a fork a few times. Place on a foil-lined baking sheet and bake for 30 to 40 minutes, or until tender. Combine the yogurt, parsley, and chives in a small bowl and season with salt and pepper to taste. Slice the potatoes in half lengthwise and top with the yogurt mixture.

Mashed Potato with Pine Nuts

SERVES 4

4 medium potatoes

2 tablespoons butter

¼ cup milk

⅓ cup toasted pine nuts

Peel potatoes and cut each into 4 even pieces. Cover with water, microwave until tender, drain, and mash well. Add butter and milk, beating until butter is melted. Add pine nuts and mix well.

TIP: Always mash potatoes when just boiled or steamed (and drained) for the best result.

Mexican Rice

SERVES 4

1 onion, chopped

14 ounces plum tomatoes, peeled and chopped

1 cup beef broth

1 cup rice

Place the onion and tomatoes in a food processor and process until smooth. Scrape the puree into a medium saucepan, add broth, and bring to a boil over medium heat. Add rice and stir once, reduce heat, cover, and simmer for 20 to 25 minutes, or until all the liquid has been absorbed and the rice is tender. Season to taste and serve immediately.

Oven-Roasted Wedges

SERVES 4 TO 6

Recipe from Cyndi O'Meara.

6 medium potatoes, unpeeled and cut into wedges

¼ cup olive oil

1 to 2 teaspoons dried oregano

Preheat the oven to 400°F. Place potatoes in a large baking dish, drizzle with oil, and coat well. Bake for 20 to 30 minutes, or until browned. Add oregano and 1 teaspoon sea salt. Toss well and serve.

Potato Pancakes

SERVES 4

These potato pancakes are shallow-fried until golden and crisp on the outside and soft on the inside.

3 medium potatoes

2 eggs, beaten

½ cup all-purpose flour

Oil, for frying

Grate potatoes and drain excess liquid. Stir in eggs, flour, and a pinch of salt. Heat oil in a nonstick skillet and add potato mixture in 2-tablespoon amounts. Cook for 5 to 10 minutes, then turn and cook for another 5 minutes. Drain on paper towels.

Potatoes Maxim

SERVES 4 TO 6

1 pound small potatoes

5 tablespoons butter, melted

Preheat the oven to 400°F. Peel and thinly slice the potatoes and place in a bowl. Add the melted butter, season with sea salt and pepper, and gently mix to coat well. Arrange the potatoes overlapping on a baking sheet. Bake for 30 minutes, or until the potatoes are cooked and browned.

OPTIONAL: Add ½ teaspoon ground cumin to the melted butter.

Red Rice

SERVES 4

8 ounces thick-cut bacon, chopped

1 can (14.5 ounces) diced tomatoes with peppers and onion

2 cups cooked rice

1 can (6 ounces) tomato paste

In a large skillet, cook bacon until nice and crispy. Add remaining ingredients with 2 cups water. Bring to a boil and cook for 3 minutes, stirring frequently. Reduce heat to a simmer, cover, and cook for 15 minutes, or until all liquid has been absorbed. Season to taste.

Rosemary & Mustard Mashed Potatoes

SERVES 4

Kim's family's favorite mash recipe!

- 2 tablespoons fresh rosemary leaves
- 4 large potatoes, peeled and cut into equal-size chunks
- 1 tablespoon Dijon mustard
- 2 tablespoons heavy cream

Boil ½ cup water with rosemary in a small saucepan. Reduce heat and simmer until infused, then drain, reserving the liquid. Boil potatoes, drain, and add rosemary liquid. Mash well, adding mustard and cream.

Rosemary & Thyme Potatoes

SERVES 4

These are lovely served with almost anything!!

- 4 large potatoes
- 2 tablespoons olive oil
- 1 tablespoon rosemary leaves, chopped
- 1 tablespoon thyme leaves

Preheat the oven to 350°F. Peel and halve the potatoes. On the non-flat side, make 4 or 5 cuts across the potatoes, slicing about three-quarters of the way through. Combine potatoes with oil in a large baking dish and sprinkle with sea salt and pepper. Bake for 20 to 30 minutes, until browned and tender. Mix herbs and sprinkle on the potatoes to serve.

Sautéed Lemon Potatoes

SERVES 4

These are sensational.

4 medium potatoes

3 tablespoons extra virgin olive oil

1 tablespoon butter

½ cup lemon juice

Preheat the oven to 350°F. Peel potatoes and cut into eighths. Cook in a pan of boiling water for 3 minutes to parboil. Drain. Combine oil, butter, and lemon juice in a baking dish and place in the oven until butter melts. Add potatoes, baste with liquid, and bake for 15 to 20 minutes, or until golden.

OPTIONAL: Add minced garlic to oil and lemon juice mixture.

Simplest Potato Bake Ever

SERVES 6

This is fabulous!!

6 potatoes

1¼ cups cream

1 envelope French onion soup mix

Preheat the oven to 350°F. Peel potatoes and cut into ⅓-inch slices. Place in a baking dish. Combine cream and soup mix. Pour over potatoes and bake for 40 minutes, or until tender.

Sweet Potato Mash with Crisp Sage Leaves

SERVES 4 TO 6

Yummy!

4 medium sweet potatoes

4 tablespoons butter

16 fresh sage leaves

Sprinkle of nutmeg

Preheat the oven to 400°F. Place sweet potatoes on a baking sheet lined with foil or parchment paper. Bake for 1 hour, until softened. When cool enough to handle, peel and set aside. Meanwhile, melt 1 tablespoon of butter in a medium skillet (be careful not to let it burn). Add sage leaves and cook for 30 seconds until crisp, then set aside. Mash sweet potatoes with remaining 3 tablespoons butter in a food processor, and season to taste. To serve, place sweet potatoes in a bowl, sprinkle with nutmeg, and top with crispy sage.

Sweet Potato Oven Fries

SERVES 4

1½ pounds sweet potatoes, peeled

1 tablespoon olive oil

½ teaspoon paprika

Preheat the oven to 400°F. Line a rimmed baking sheet or a large roasting pan with parchment paper. Halve the sweet potatoes crosswise, then cut lengthwise into ½-inch-wide wedges. Place on the baking sheet. Toss with oil and paprika and season with pepper. Bake, turning twice, for 20 minutes, or until golden brown and tender.

Taters & Onions

SERVES 4

3 to 4 large potatoes

2½ tablespoons bacon fat

1 large onion, halved and sliced

Peel potatoes and slice into french fry shapes. As you work, place potatoes in a bowl of cold water to cover to prevent discoloration. Heat fat in a skillet over medium-high heat until hot. Drain potatoes and pat dry with paper towels. Put potatoes, onion, and salt and pepper to taste in skillet. Cover and cook without turning for 5 to 10 minutes, or until they are browned on one side. Uncover, turn potatoes, and cook another 5 to 10 minutes, or until nicely browned all over.

VEGETABLES

Asparagus with Balsamic Dressing
SERVES 4

2 bunches asparagus

¼ cup olive oil

¼ cup balsamic vinegar

2 vine-ripened tomatoes, diced

Preheat the broiler. Brush the asparagus with some of the oil, then broil for 5 minutes, or until tender. Serve drizzled with combined remaining oil, vinegar, and diced tomato.

OPTIONAL: For extra flavor, sprinkle with 2 tablespoons finely chopped basil leaves.

Asparagus with Butter & Parmesan
SERVES 4

2 bunches asparagus

2 tablespoons butter, melted

½ cup shaved Parmesan cheese

Bring water to a boil in a large skillet. Add asparagus, simmer uncovered for 2 minutes, and then drain. Drizzle with melted butter and sprinkle with sea salt, pepper, and Parmesan.

Bacon-Stuffed Mushrooms

SERVES 4

4 large stuffer mushrooms (large white or small portobellos)

4 slices bacon

½ cup seasoned bread crumbs

¾ cup shredded mozzarella cheese

Preheat the oven to 350°F. Remove mushroom stems. Cut bacon into fine strips and lightly fry. Mix bread crumbs and cheese together and add bacon. Place mushrooms, stem side up, on a nonstick baking sheet. Spoon mixture onto the mushrooms, season, and bake for 15 minutes.

Baked Sweet Squash

SERVES 4

4 small acorn squash

4 teaspoons butter

4 teaspoons brown sugar

2 teaspoons ground cinnamon

Preheat the oven to 375°F. Cut off the top third of the squash and scrape out all the seeds. Combine butter and brown sugar and spoon mixture into each squash. Sprinkle with cinnamon and put the lid back on. Place in a baking pan with ¾ inch of water in the bottom. Bake for 30 minutes, or until tender.

Beans with Garlic & Pine Nuts

SERVES 4

These are scrumptious!

½ pound green beans, trimmed

3 tablespoons olive oil

1 or 2 cloves garlic, halved

¼ cup pine nuts, toasted

Microwave beans (with a little water) for 1 minute, then drain. Heat oil and garlic in a skillet over low heat until garlic just changes color. Add beans, sauté for a minute, then add pine nuts and stir until heated through.

TIP: Toast pine nuts on a baking sheet in a 350°F oven for 3 minutes.

Beer-Battered Onion Rings

SERVES 4

4 cups sunflower oil

1 cup all-purpose flour

1 cup strong beer

4 onions, sliced into rings

In a large, deep skillet, heat oil to 365°F. Meanwhile, in a bowl, combine flour, beer, and salt and pepper to taste. Mix until smooth. Dredge onion slices in the batter until evenly coated. Deep-fry in the hot oil until golden brown. Drain on paper towels.

Boston Baked Beans

SERVES 6

2 cups dried cannellini or pinto beans, rinsed and picked over

1 small ham hock

1 onion, diced

½ cup molasses

Place beans in a bowl, cover with water, and soak overnight. Drain. Fill a large saucepan with water and add beans, ham hock, and onion. Bring to a boil, cover, reduce to a high simmer, and cook for 45 minutes, or until beans are semi-tender. Watch that the water remains above the beans; you may need to top it up. Remove from the heat and stir in the molasses. Preheat the oven to 300°F. Pour mixture into a baking dish and season. Bury the ham hock in the beans, slightly exposing the rind for further color. Cover and bake for about 4 hours. The end result should be that the water evaporates and a thick, delicious sauce remains. Pull the meat from the hock and stir into the beans.

TIP: This can be served as a side or as a main meal with fresh, crusty bread and seasonal veggies.

Brussels Sprouts & Bacon

SERVES 4

20 brussels sprouts

4 slices bacon, diced

1 tablespoon hazelnut oil

Cut a crisscross into the base of the sprouts. Cook the sprouts in a saucepan of boiling water for about 8 minutes, or until tender. Drain and transfer to a serving bowl. Fry bacon until crisp and add to sprouts along with hazelnut oil.

Cheesy Peas

SERVES 4

Peas and Parmesan—a delicious combination.

1 pound frozen peas

2½ tablespoons butter

1 tablespoon lemon juice

⅓ cup shredded Parmesan cheese

Microwave peas, butter, and lemon juice on high for 1 minute. Remove, stir, and microwave for 2 minutes longer. Let stand, covered, for 2 to 3 minutes. Transfer to a serving dish and sprinkle with Parmesan. Serve immediately.

Corn Dumplings

MAKES ABOUT 24

These delicious dumplings cook on top of a stew or casserole.

1 cup self-rising flour

1 cup polenta or cornmeal

5 tablespoons butter, softened

1 can (8 ounces) corn kernels

Place flour and polenta in a bowl and rub in butter. Add corn and juice from the can to make a soft, sticky dough. To use, place tablespoons of dough on top of a simmering stew. Re-cover and continue cooking (or baking) for about 20 minutes.

OPTIONAL: Serve with a yummy casserole or stew, or on our delicious Chili con Carne (page 111).

Crunchy Snow Peas

SERVES 4

Thanks, Michelle Dodd, for this terrific little tip!

1 pound snow peas

Top and tail snow peas and place in a heatproof, sealable container. Boil a kettle of water. Cover peas with boiling water, seal the container, and let stand for 3 minutes. Drain and serve.

Fried Green Tomatoes

SERVES 6 TO 8

1 cup cornmeal

¼ cup grated Parmesan cheese

6 large green tomatoes, cut into ¼-inch-thick slices

¼ cup olive oil

Combine cornmeal and Parmesan and season with salt and pepper. Coat tomatoes in cornmeal mix. In a large nonstick skillet, heat oil over medium heat. Add tomatoes and cook until golden brown on one side, 3 to 4 minutes. Flip and fry the other side.

Garlic Mushrooms

SERVES 4

1 pound button mushrooms, stemmed

2 tablespoons olive oil

1 or 2 cloves garlic, crushed

¼ cup minced flat-leaf parsley

Preheat the oven to 350°F. Place the mushrooms in a large baking dish, drizzle with oil and garlic, and bake for 15 minutes, or until tender and lightly browned. Stir in parsley.

TIP: Cook close to serving.

Grilled Corn with Parmesan & Cayenne

SERVES 4

4 ears of corn, unhusked

2 tablespoons mayonnaise

2 tablespoons grated Parmesan cheese

½ teaspoon cayenne pepper

Preheat the oven to 350°F. Place the unhusked corn in the oven and roast for 20 minutes, until the corn is soft when you press on it. Meanwhile, preheat a grill to high. Pull the husks down (but do not take off) and remove the corn silk. Tie each husk in a knot so you can hold on to it like a handle. Char the corn on the grill until the kernels are slightly blackened all around and start popping (about 6 minutes). Rub the corn all over with mayonnaise and sprinkle with Parmesan and cayenne.

OPTIONAL: Serve with lime wedges.

Honey & Mustard Roast Parsnips

SERVES 6 TO 8

Parsnips are just lovely roasted—give them a try!

2¼ pounds parsnips, quartered

¼ cup extra virgin olive oil

3 tablespoons honey

4 tablespoons whole-grain mustard

Preheat the oven to 400°F. Cook parsnips in lightly salted boiling water for 5 minutes. Drain, then place them in a large roasting pan, add oil, and toss to coat well. Roast for 40 minutes, or until crispy. Mix the honey and mustard and spread over the parsnips, then roast for 5 minutes longer.

Honey Carrots

SERVES 4 TO 6

1 pound baby carrots

1 tablespoon honey

2 teaspoons butter

In a saucepan, bring ½ cup water to a boil. Add carrots, return to a boil, cover, and steam for 10 minutes. Drain any remaining water and toss carrots with honey and butter.

Lemon Broccoli

SERVES 4 TO 6

Recipe from Cyndi O'Meara.

1 head broccoli, cut into medium-size florets

1 tablespoon lemon juice

In a medium saucepan, bring 1 cup water to a boil. Add broccoli, return to a boil, and simmer for 3 minutes. Remove from heat and drain. Drizzle with lemon juice before serving.

Minted Pea Mash

SERVES 4

Great with steak.

1 pound red-skinned potatoes, peeled and chopped

3 cups frozen peas

⅓ cup milk

⅓ cup chopped mint leaves

Cook potatoes in a large saucepan of boiling water until soft. Add peas and cook for 5 minutes. Drain and cool slightly. Return peas and potatoes to the pan, add milk, and mash with a potato masher until almost smooth. Mix in mint leaves. Season well with salt and pepper.

Oven-Baked Tomatoes

SERVES 3

Yummy!

3 vine-ripened tomatoes

3 teaspoons pesto

3 tablespoons grated Parmesan cheese

Preheat the oven to 400°F. Halve tomatoes and place cut sides up in a baking dish. Season each with sea salt and pepper. Smooth pesto over each and top with Parmesan. Bake for 20 minutes, or until soft.

Rich Grits

SERVES 4 TO 6

1¾ cups hominy grits or white cornmeal

3 tablespoons butter, softened

4 ounces Cheddar cheese, grated

Cook grits according to package directions. Stir in butter and cheese and season to taste. Beat really well, until quite creamy. Allow to sit for 5 minutes. Serve.

OPTIONAL: This is yummy served with fried shrimp and sausages.

Roasted Beets

SERVES 4 TO 6

1 bunch beets

Preheat the oven to 350°F. Wash the beets well and trim the leaves, leaving about 1 inch of stalk. Remove most of the root but not all. Do not peel. Wrap well in foil and bake for 40 minutes, or until tender. Unwrap and peel.

OPTIONAL: Season with black pepper and butter or horseradish cream and serve with salmon. . . . *Mmmmm!*

Sautéed Asparagus

SERVES 4

¼ cup olive oil

2 bunches asparagus, trimmed

Heat a heavy skillet and douse with olive oil. Reduce the heat and sauté asparagus until cooked. Season lightly with sea salt and pepper.

Snow Peas in Garlic-Mint Butter

SERVES 8

8 ounces snow peas

1½ tablespoons butter

2 cloves garlic, crushed

1 teaspoon chopped mint

Top and tail snow peas. Melt butter in a skillet and then add garlic and mint. Stir in peas and sauté until just tender.

Steamed Broccoli Scattered with Pine Nuts

SERVES 4

1 to 2 large stalks broccoli, separated into florets

1 to 2 tablespoons butter

¼ cup pine nuts, toasted

Steam broccoli until just tender and still bright green. Place in a serving dish, dot with butter, scatter with pine nuts, and sprinkle with black pepper.

Stuffed Peppers

SERVES 8

4 red bell peppers, cut in half

1 pound ground beef

1 medium onion, finely diced

2 celery stalks, finely diced

Preheat the oven to 300°F. Scrape out peppers and set aside. In a skillet, cook beef, onion, and celery, and season generously with black pepper and a little sea salt. Spoon into pepper halves and place on a foil-lined baking sheet. Bake for 30 minutes. Serve hot.

OPTIONAL: Sprinkle with a little Cheddar cheese before baking.

Tempura Batter

MAKES 1½ CUPS

Use for small cut vegetables and meats and shallow-fry.

⅔ cup all-purpose flour

⅓ cup cornstarch

9 ounces very cold seltzer or club soda

Sift flour and cornstarch into a bowl and add a pinch of sea salt. Make a well in the center and add seltzer, mixing well until smooth and lump free. Set aside for 10 to 15 minutes before using.

White Bean Puree

SERVES 4

1 can (15 ounces) cannellini beans, rinsed and drained

¼ cup almond meal

1 tablespoon lemon juice

1 clove garlic, crushed

Place all ingredients in a food processor and blend until smooth. This can be served as a dip or as a side to chicken or fish.

OPTIONAL: Serve drizzled finely with a little olive oil for presentation.

Zucchini Hash Browns

MAKES 4

1 cup grated zucchini

2 eggs, lightly beaten

Mixed herb seasoning to taste

2 tablespoons olive oil

In a medium bowl, mix zucchini, eggs, and seasoning. Heat oil in a heavy skillet and gently drop zucchini mixture by the tablespoon into the hot oil. When brown on one side, turn over and cook on the other side. Stack on a plate and keep warm until the whole batch is cooked.

OPTIONAL: Top with Thai sweet chili sauce, sour cream, or butter.

MAINS

The opinions expressed by the man of this house are not necessarily those of the management.

—Anonymous

BEEF

Beef Patties
SERVES 4

A recipe from the delightful Rebecca Butler.

1 pound lean ground beef

1 cup mashed potatoes

¼ cup finely chopped onion

3 tablespoons extra virgin olive oil

Combine beef, potatoes, and onion in a bowl. Season with sea salt and pepper. Form into patties. In a skillet, heat oil. Add patties and cook, turning occasionally, until browned and crusty on both sides.

OPTIONAL: Serve with gravy and vegetables.

Beef Stir-fry
SERVES 4

Quick, easy, and delicious.

⅔ cup barbecue sauce

1 pound beef, cut for stir-fry

2 tablespoons sesame oil

4 to 6 scallions

Mix barbecue sauce and meat together and let stand for 15 minutes. Heat oil in a wok or skillet. In batches, stir-fry meat for 1 minute, or until cooked on the outside and medium on the inside. Transfer the meat to a bowl as you work. Trim scallions and cut into thin lengthwise strips. Quickly stir-fry in the wok. Serve meat topped with scallions and sauce.

OPTIONAL: Serve on top of a salad. Even just shredded iceberg lettuce is nice.

Beef Stroganoff

SERVES 4

Another simple main for a quick and easy dinner.

1 pound beef, cut for stir-fry

2 cups button mushrooms, halved

1 envelope beef Stroganoff seasoning

1 cup sour cream

In a nonstick skillet, brown beef. Transfer to a plate. Add 2 tablespoons water and mushrooms to skillet and cook for 5 minutes. Return beef to skillet and sprinkle with salt and pepper. Mix Stroganoff seasoning with 1 cup water, add to skillet, and bring to a boil. Reduce heat, cover, and simmer for 2 hours, or until meat is tender. Taste and adjust seasonings. Stir in sour cream and serve hot.

OPTIONAL: Serve over rice or pasta.

Chili con Carne

SERVES 8

3¼ pounds chuck steak, cut into cubes

2 cans (14.5 ounces each) diced tomatoes with peppers and onions

3 tablespoons Mexican seasoning blend

1 can (15 ounces) red kidney beans, rinsed and drained

Heat a deep nonstick skillet and cook beef in batches until browned on the outside. Return meat to pan and add tomatoes, seasoning blend, and 1 cup water. Bring to a boil, reduce heat to a simmer, cover, and cook for 2½ hours. Slow-cooking this cut of meat tenderizes it. Using two forks, coarsely shred one-fourth of the meat. Return shredded meat to pan and add beans. If the sauce is too thin, continue to simmer, uncovered, until reduced. Season and serve.

OPTIONAL: This is nice served with Corn Dumplings (page 97) steamed on top.

Coffee- & Pepper-Crusted Steaks

SERVES 4

This is charmingly unusual!

2 tablespoons whole coffee beans

2 tablespoons whole black peppercorns

4 rib eye steaks, 2 inches thick (2 pounds total)

Extra virgin olive oil for brushing on steaks

Preheat a broiler or grill to high. Coarsely grind the coffee beans and peppercorns. Press the mixture evenly into both sides of the steaks. Brush steaks lightly with oil. Broil or grill the steaks, turning once halfway through grilling time (do not turn steaks until you see beads of juice on the surface), for 10 minutes, or until desired degree of doneness. Remove the steaks from the grill and season both sides with sea salt. Allow to rest for 2 to 3 minutes before serving.

Coney Island Burgers

MAKES 4

1 pound lean ground beef

½ cup barbecue sauce

¼ cup pickle relish

½ onion, finely diced

Combine all ingredients and form into 4 patties. Over medium-high heat, grill for 4 minutes on each side, or until browned and cooked through.

OPTIONAL: Serve on a crusty roll with mustard, lettuce, and tomato. Or make mini burgers for yummy sliders.

Corned Beef

SERVES 6

2 pounds corned beef

6 whole cloves

⅓ cup maple syrup

Place meat in a large pot and cover with water. Bring to a boil, reduce heat to a simmer, add cloves, and cook for 1 hour, or until tender. Preheat the oven to 350°F. When cooked, drain corned beef (reserving cloves) and place in a shallow baking dish. Press cloves into meat, drizzle with syrup, and dust with freshly cracked pepper. Bake in a 350°F oven for 15 minutes to glaze.

Creamy Meatballs

SERVES 4 TO 6

1½ pounds extra-lean ground beef

1 cup sour cream

1 teaspoon garlic salt

2 tablespoons olive oil

Combine beef, sour cream, and garlic salt. Roll into 1½- to 1¾-inch meatballs. Heat oil in a nonstick skillet. Drop in meatballs and fry for 15 minutes over medium heat, until they are browned all over. Place the balls on paper towels to drain off excess oil before serving.

OPTIONAL: Roll in bread crumbs before cooking.

Creole Pepper Steaks

SERVES 6

A mouthwatering mix of flavors.

2 cloves garlic, crushed

1 teaspoon dried thyme

1 teaspoon paprika

6 sirloin steaks, 1 inch thick

Combine garlic, thyme, paprika, and cracked black pepper. Coat the steaks evenly, pressing the seasonings into each side. Over medium-high heat, grill each side for 4 to 5 minutes for medium; flip only once. Remove and let rest for 5 minutes before serving.

Easy Roast Beef

SERVES 4 TO 6

A recipe from Shane McCosker. This is a sensational Sunday roast and soooooooooo easy!

2-pound beef rib roast

1 envelope French onion soup mix

1 can (10.75 ounces) condensed cream of mushroom soup

Preheat the oven to 350°F. Place a large sheet of foil (big enough to fully wrap the beef) in an ovenproof skillet. Place beef in the center of the foil and bring foil up to form a bowl. Combine soups in a mixing bowl. Mix thoroughly and pour over beef. Fold foil to seal tightly. Bake for 1 hour, or until tender. Serve with the delicious gravy in the bottom of the foil bag.

OPTIONAL: Serve with your family's favorite roast vegetables.

Garlic Roast Beef

SERVES 4

2 pounds lean beef for roasting

1 bulb garlic, separated into cloves, each clove peeled and halved

5 tablespoons olive oil

1 tablespoon lemon-pepper seasoning

Place beef in a shallow roasting pan lined with parchment paper. Using a sharp knife, pierce the roast at 1-inch intervals so you have slits long enough to house a halved garlic clove in each. Drizzle about 1 tablespoon oil over beef and rub with lemon-pepper. Cover with plastic wrap and marinate in the refrigerator for at least 2 hours. Preheat the oven to 400°F. Drizzle the remaining ¼ cup oil over beef and place in the oven. Reduce the heat to 350°F and slow-cook for 3½ hours.

TIP: Leftover meat makes an excellent sandwich. Layer thinly sliced roast beef onto your favorite bread with some Tabasco sauce, lightly sautéed onions, and sliced tomato.

Glen's Corned Beef

SERVES 6

A recipe perfected by Glen, Kim's husband.

2 pounds corned beef

5 cups ginger ale

Place meat in a large pot, add the ginger ale, and simmer, partially covered, for 1 hour (skim fat from surface and discard), or until tender.

OPTIONAL: Serve with vegetables and horseradish sauce.

Massaman Curry

SERVES 4

Served up regularly in the Bermingham household!

1 pound lean beef, cut for stir-fry

1 tablespoon Massaman curry paste

1 can (14 ounces) coconut milk

3 red-skinned potatoes, peeled and cubed

Place beef and ¼ cup water in a nonstick skillet or large saucepan. Cook over high heat until browned. Combine curry paste and coconut milk and add to beef. Add potatoes, turn down to very lowest heat, and simmer for 30 minutes, or until potatoes are cooked through.

OPTIONAL: Can add ½ cup cashews and serve with rice.

Pan-fried Steak

SERVES 2

Mouthwatering.

1 tablespoon olive oil

1 tablespoon butter

2 sirloin or New York strip steaks (1½ inches thick)

In a large skillet, heat oil and butter over high heat. Reduce heat to medium-high and immediately add steaks. Cook for 6 to 7 minutes on one side, then turn and cook another 6 to 7 minutes, until caramelized on the outside and still pink in the center when cut (medium). Transfer to warm plates and let rest for 5 minutes before enjoying.

Pesto-Stuffed Steaks

SERVES 4

F.A.S.T & F.A.B.U.L.O.U.S!

- 2 beef rib eye steaks, about 1¼ inches thick
- ¼ cup pesto
- 3 tablespoons shaved Parmesan cheese
- 1 tablespoon extra virgin olive oil

Cut into the side of each steak, forming a deep pocket (do not cut through). Mix pesto and cheese and spread into pockets. Press closed, securing with a toothpick, and drizzle oil over beef. Preheat a heavy skillet until the pan is hot. Place steaks carefully in the pan and cook for 8 to 10 minutes for medium, turning once when you see juices on the surface of the steak. When done, remove, cover, and let stand for 5 minutes. Cut beef into thick strips to serve.

Potpie
SERVES 2

*This is the perfect meal to serve up
while watching Monday Night Football.*

½ onion, peeled and finely chopped

1 pound lean ground beef

8 ounces fruit chutney

½ sheet puff pastry

Preheat the oven to 375°F. Place onion in a nonstick skillet with ½ cup water and cook over medium heat for 5 minutes. Add beef and cook until browned, then add chutney. Stir until heated through. Spoon mixture into two 4-inch-diameter ramekins. Cut 2 rounds of puff pastry to fit tops of ramekins and top pie with pastry, pressing edges to the rim with a fork. Bake for 15 to 20 minutes, or until pastry top is golden.

Quick Meat Loaf

SERVES 4

Serve hot with vegetables, salad, or mashed potatoes.
This is also great to freeze.

1 pound extra-lean ground beef

3 eggs, lightly beaten

¾ cup bread crumbs

5 tablespoons tomato paste

Preheat the oven to 350°F. Line a loaf pan with parchment paper. Mix beef, eggs, bread crumbs, and 4 tablespoons of tomato paste together and place in the loaf pan. Spread remaining 1 tablespoon tomato paste on top of meat loaf. Bake for 50 minutes, or until lightly browned on top.

OPTIONAL: For more zing add 1 teaspoon curry powder. To get your five-vegetable quota for the day, add shredded carrot, diced sweet potato, diced mushrooms, peas, and corn to the mix before baking.

Rissoles

MAKES 8

From playgroup chef extraordinaire, Aine Watkins!

1 pound extra-lean ground beef

2 medium onions, diced

2 medium eggs

¼ cup all-purpose flour

Preheat a panini press or electric grill. Mix beef, onions, and eggs and season with salt and pepper. Divide into 8 portions and roll into balls. Roll in flour. Place in between the grill plates and cook until done.

Roast Beef with Horseradish Cream

SERVES 6

2 tablespoons olive oil

2 pounds beef rib roast

½ teaspoon dried thyme

1 cup Horseradish Cream (page 46)

Preheat the oven to 300°F. Lightly oil the roast and sear it in a nonstick skillet over moderately high heat for 2 to 3 minutes, or until evenly browned all over. In a small bowl, combine thyme with 1 teaspoon each of sea salt and pepper. Place the roast in a large shallow roasting pan and sprinkle with the seasoning mix. Roast in the lower third of your oven for 2 to 2¼ hours. Transfer to a carving board and cover loosely with foil. Let stand for 15 minutes. Carve and serve with Horseradish Cream.

TIP: For a medium roast, the internal temperature is between 140° and 145°F; or when gently squeezed with tongs, the meat is springy but soft.

Salsa Patties

SERVES 6

A recipe from the beautiful Rebecca Butler.

1½ pounds lean ground beef

⅓ cup salsa

1 cup crushed Ritz crackers

2 tablespoons olive oil

Combine beef, salsa, and cracker crumbs. Shape into 6 patties. In a large nonstick skillet, heat 1 tablespoon oil over medium-high heat. Add half the patties and cook for about 5 minutes on each side, or until nicely browned and cooked through. Drain on paper towels. Repeat with remaining oil and patties.

OPTIONAL: Delicious served with rice, salad, and a dollop of guacamole.

Sloppy Joes

SERVES 4

Soooo nice!

1 pound lean ground beef

½ onion, chopped

½ green bell pepper, chopped

¾ cup ketchup

In a nonstick skillet, brown beef, onion, and bell pepper over medium heat. Season with salt and pepper. Stir in ketchup and mix thoroughly. Reduce heat and simmer for 20 minutes.

OPTIONAL: Add 1 tablespoon dry mustard.

CHICKEN & TURKEY

The more we share, the more we have.

—Anonymous

Apricot Chicken

SERVES 4

8 skinless, bone-in chicken pieces

1 envelope French onion soup mix

1 onion, diced

2 cups apricot nectar

Preheat the oven to 350°F. Place chicken pieces in a baking dish with soup mix and onion and season with sea salt and pepper. Add apricot nectar and stir. Cover and bake for 1½ hours.

OPTIONAL: For a change, place chicken in a plastic bag, coat with flour, salt, and pepper, and lightly sauté. Add the other ingredients and bake for only 1 hour.

Buffalo Wings

SERVES 8

OMG . . . These are good!

4 to 5 pounds chicken wings

4 cups vegetable oil

¼ cup (½ stick) butter

5 tablespoons Louisiana-style hot sauce (Durkee or Crystal)

Chop the tip off each wing and discard. Cut the wing in two at the joint to make two pieces. Heat the oil over high heat in a deep skillet, Dutch oven, or deep-fryer until it starts to pop and sizzle (around 400°F). In two batches, add the chicken pieces and cook until they're crisp, stirring occasionally. Drain on paper towels. Melt butter in a heavy saucepan and add hot sauce. Stir well and remove from the heat immediately. Place the chicken on a warm serving platter, pour the sauce on top, and serve.

OPTIONAL: To be authentic, we've been told to accompany the hot wings with crisp fresh celery and Blue Cheese Dressing (page 71), both of which are said to help *ease the heat* of the hot wings.

Cajun Chicken Kebabs

SERVES 2

Light and luscious with a simple salad!

10 ounces skinless, boneless chicken breast, cubed

1 red bell pepper, cut into chunks

1 onion, cut into chunks

2 tablespoons Cajun seasoning blend

Coat grill racks with cooking spray. Preheat the grill to high. Soak bamboo skewers in water, then thread chicken, bell pepper, and onion onto them. Sprinkle with seasoning. Grill for 2 to 3 minutes on each side, or until cooked through.

Cheese & Prosciutto Chicken

SERVES 4

Another great recipe from Wendy Beattie's vibrant kitchen.

4 skinless, boneless chicken breast halves (6 ounces each)

4 slices Swiss cheese

8 slices prosciutto

2 tablespoons extra virgin olive oil

Preheat the oven to 400°F. Make a lengthwise slit in the thicker side of each breast to make a pocket, leaving ⅓ inch at each end. Fill each pocket with 1 slice cheese and 2 slices prosciutto and seal opening with a toothpick. Heat oil in a large nonstick skillet over medium-high heat. Add chicken and cook for 1 to 2 minutes, until golden on each side. Transfer to a rimmed baking sheet and roast for 7 to 10 minutes, or until cooked through. Cover and set aside to rest for 5 minutes.

OPTIONAL: Serve with sweet potato mash and baby spinach.

Chicken & Jarlsberg Casserole
SERVES 6

A sensational recipe by Julie McDonald.

6 skinless, boneless chicken breast halves (6 ounces each)

6 slices Jarlsberg cheese

1 can (10.75 ounces) condensed cream of chicken soup

⅓ cup milk

Preheat the oven to 325°F. Place chicken in a baking dish and cover with cheese. Mix soup and milk and pour over chicken. Season with pepper. Bake, uncovered, for 1 hour.

Chicken, Butternut & Chickpea Curry
SERVES 6

1½ pounds butternut squash

2 pounds skinless, boneless chicken thighs

1 can (10.5 ounces) chickpeas, rinsed and drained

1 jar (15 ounces) korma curry cooking sauce

Halve and seed the butternut squash. Wrap in plastic wrap and microwave on high for 5 to 6 minutes, or until almost cooked. Peel and cut into cubes. Cut chicken thighs in half. Place chicken, squash, chickpeas, and curry sauce in a saucepan. Wash curry sauce jar with about ¼ cup hot water and add to the saucepan. Cover and cook over medium heat for 30 minutes, or until chicken is cooked through.

Chicken Enchiladas

MAKES 12

FANTASTIC . . . The kids will looove them!

12 flour tortillas

1½ cups shredded cooked chicken, home-roasted or rotisserie

2 cups shredded mozzarella cheese or queso blanco

1 can (28 ounces) red enchilada sauce

Preheat the oven to 375°F. Warm tortillas in the microwave for 30 seconds, or until soft. Divide the chicken among the tortillas, roll up, and place in a baking dish seam side down. Top tortillas with half the cheese. Pour sauce over and top with remaining cheese. Bake for 30 minutes, or until the cheese is golden and bubbling.

OPTIONAL: Add some chopped onion and peppers with the chicken.

Chicken Marsala

SERVES 4

Elegant, easy, and delicious.

4 skinless, boneless chicken breast halves (6 ounces each)

8 ounces mushrooms, sliced

½ cup marsala wine

½ cup heavy cream

Flatten the chicken with a meat pounder. In a large nonstick skillet, cook chicken in 2 tablespoons water for 15 minutes, or until just cooked. Push to the side, add mushrooms, and cook until soft. Add marsala wine and bring to a boil. Boil for 2 to 3 minutes. Season with sea salt and pepper. Stir in cream and simmer for 4 minutes, or until heated through.

Chicken Pie

SERVES 4 TO 6

This redefines fast and fabulous.

2 sheets puff pastry

1 can (10.75 ounces) condensed cream of chicken soup

1 cup cooked chicken, cubed

2 cups frozen mixed veggies, thawed

Preheat the oven to 350°F. Line a 10-inch pie plate with parchment paper. Place 1 sheet of puff pastry in it. Combine remaining ingredients in a bowl, season with salt and pepper, and pour into pastry. Cover with the remaining sheet, and seal edges well by pressing with a fork. Cut several slits in the pie lid and bake for 30 minutes, or until lid is golden brown.

OPTIONAL: Brush with beaten egg or milk for a very presentable finish. This is best made a couple of hours ahead of serving.

Chicken Schnitzel

SERVES 4

A family favorite!

¼ cup olive oil

4 breaded chicken cutlets (5 ounces each)

1 cup herbed pasta sauce

1 cup shredded mozzarella cheese

Preheat the broiler. Heat a large nonstick skillet and add oil. When hot, add cutlets and cook until golden brown on both sides. Place on a foil-lined broiler pan. Top evenly with pasta sauce and cheese. Broil until cheese is bubbling and golden.

Chicken Tikka Masala

SERVES 4

This is just soooo goood—try it!

- 1½ pounds skinless, boneless chicken breasts, cut into chunks
- 2 tablespoons tikka masala curry paste
- 1 can (10.75 ounces) condensed cream of tomato soup
- 2 to 3 tablespoons plain yogurt

Heat a nonstick skillet, add the chicken, and cook for 5 to 6 minutes, or until browned. (If chicken starts to stick, add 1 to 2 tablespoons water.) Add the curry paste, soup, and ¼ cup water (see Tip) and simmer for 15 minutes. Stir in the yogurt and heat through.

OPTIONAL: Serve with rice and garnish with cilantro.

TIP: Use the ¼ cup water to rinse the inside of the soup can so you get every last drop of soup.

Chutney Chicken Dish

SERVES 2

This is deliciously simple!

- 2 tablespoons fruit chutney
- 2 tablespoons Dijon mustard
- 2 skinless, boneless chicken breast halves (6 ounces each)
- ¼ cup grated Cheddar cheese

Preheat the oven to 350°F. Mix the chutney with the mustard and cover the chicken breasts. Place chicken breasts in a baking dish, cover with cheese, and bake for 15 to 20 minutes, or until the chicken is cooked through and the cheese is golden and bubbling.

OPTIONAL: Serve with rice or vegetables.

Classic Turkey Gravy

MAKES ABOUT 3 CUPS

Chicken or turkey stock

½ cup (1 stick) butter

⅔ cup all-purpose flour

Drain the pan drippings from the roasted turkey. Let sit and then remove any fat from the top. Pour the drippings into a 4-cup measure and add enough chicken stock to make 4 cups. In a medium saucepan, melt butter and season with cracked pepper. Over medium-low heat, add flour and cook, constantly whisking to avoid lumps, for about 3 minutes. Slowly add stock and cook, whisking constantly, for about 3 minutes, or until bubbling and thick. Use right away or keep warm over lowest heat setting. Whisk again before serving.

Corn Bread Stuffing

SERVES 6 TO 8

Scrummy served with turkey as a side dish.

5¼ cups chicken broth

3 celery stalks, chopped

¼ cup chopped canned water chestnuts

1 bag (16 ounces) herb-seasoned corn bread stuffing mix

In a large skillet, heat chicken broth over medium heat. Add celery and water chestnuts, cover with a generous amount of pepper, and stir over medium heat until it comes to a rolling boil. Reduce heat to low, cover, and simmer 5 to 7 minutes. Remove the skillet from the heat and carefully fold herb-seasoned stuffing mix into the broth until it is well blended (should be moist).

Green Chicken Curry

SERVES 4

Now, this is flavor!

¼ cup Thai green curry paste

1¼ pounds skinless, boneless chicken thighs, cut into strips

1 can (14 ounces) coconut cream

1 cup cut green beans (2-inch pieces)

Heat a wok or large skillet. Add green curry paste, cooking and stirring for 1 minute, or until fragrant. Add chicken and cook, stirring, for 10 minutes, until almost done. Stir in coconut cream and bring to a boil. Simmer, uncovered, for 20 minutes. Add beans and simmer for 10 minutes, or until just tender.

OPTIONAL: We often add more vegetables and serve with rice to soak up the delicious sauce.

Grilled Chicken with Roasted Peppers & Tomato Sauce

SERVES 4

4 red bell peppers, halved

8 skinless chicken drumsticks

¼ cup sun-dried tomato pesto

1 large tomato, seeded and cubed

Preheat the broiler. Place peppers, cut side down, and chicken on a foil-lined broiler pan. Broil until skin on the peppers starts to blister and until juices run clear from chicken, 15 to 20 minutes. Remove skin from peppers and blend peppers with pesto until smooth. Serve chicken with puree, topped with tomato.

Honey Mustard Chicken Breasts

SERVES 4

D.E.L.E.C.T.A.B.L.E.

4 skinless, boneless chicken breast halves (about 6 ounces each)

½ cup honey

½ cup Dijon mustard

1 teaspoon paprika

Preheat the broiler. Gently pound the chicken breasts to even out. Sprinkle with sea salt and pepper to taste. Mix remaining ingredients, pour half of this mixture over the chicken, and brush to coat. Broil, basting regularly with remaining honey-mustard mixture, for 15 to 20 minutes, or until chicken is no longer pink and juices run clear. Let cool 10 minutes before serving.

Honey-Baked Chicken

SERVES 4 TO 6

1 envelope French onion soup mix

3 tablespoons honey

¾ cup white wine or water

2¼ pounds chicken pieces

Preheat the oven to 350°F. Combine soup mix, honey, and white wine (or water) and pour evenly over chicken pieces in a shallow baking dish. Cover and bake for 1 hour. Uncover and bake for another 30 minutes.

Indian Chicken Curry

SERVES 4 TO 6

Very easy and very yummy!

1 rotisserie chicken

1 cup plain yogurt

6 tablespoons mayonnaise

2 tablespoons curry powder

Cut chicken into bite-size pieces. In a bowl, mix together yogurt, mayonnaise, and curry powder. Place chicken in a baking dish, add yogurt mixture, and toss to coat. Refrigerate and let marinate for at least 1 hour. Preheat the oven to 350°F. Bake chicken for 10 to 12 minutes, or until warmed through.

OPTIONAL: Serve with rice, fresh cilantro, and lemon wedges.

Kazza's Wonderful Chicken

SERVES 2

A recipe from Karyn Turnbull.

2 skinless, boneless chicken breast halves (6 ounces each)

½ cup sour cream

¼ cup slivered almonds

½ cup grated Jarlsberg cheese

Preheat the oven to 325°F. Dip breasts into sour cream. Mix almonds and Jarlsberg together and then roll chicken in this, coating well. Place in a shallow baking dish and bake for 20 minutes, or until chicken is golden brown.

Mascarpone & Cilantro Chicken

SERVES 4

A super recipe from Janelle McCosker.

2 tablespoons olive oil

1½ pounds skinless, boneless chicken thighs, quartered

2 ounces mascarpone cheese

½ cup chopped cilantro

Heat oil in a nonstick skillet, add chicken, and cook until golden, turning occasionally. Add mascarpone and stir until melted and simmering. Add cilantro and mix well. Remove from the heat and season with sea salt and pepper. Serve drizzled with the yummy sauce.

OPTIONAL: Accompany with fresh, leafy greens.

Mexican Chicken

SERVES 4

This is yummy.

4 skinless, boneless chicken breast halves (6 ounces each)

1 envelope taco seasoning

2 cups salsa

2 tablespoons sour cream

In a nonstick skillet over medium-high heat, add 2 tablespoons water and chicken and cook for 3 to 4 minutes, or until chicken is browned. Reduce heat, add taco seasoning and salsa, and simmer for 15 minutes, or until the chicken is cooked through. Stir in sour cream.

Pesto & Chicken Parcels

SERVES 4

These are fabulous.

4 skinless, boneless chicken thighs (5 ounces each)

4 tablespoons pesto

4 ounces Camembert cheese

2 sheets puff pastry

Preheat the oven to 350°F. Open chicken thighs and lay them flat. Coat with pesto and season with sea salt and pepper. Cut cheese into thin strips and cover chicken. Start from one end of the chicken thigh and roll it up. Cut each sheet of puff pastry flat on the diagonal. Place a chicken thigh in the middle and fold to cover, sealing the edges with a fork. Place on a baking sheet and bake for 30 minutes.

Pesto Chicken

SERVES 4

4 skinless, boneless chicken breast halves (6 ounces each)

1 tablespoon olive oil

3 tablespoons pesto

8 thin slices mozzarella cheese

Preheat the broiler. Pound chicken breasts to flatten slightly. Heat oil in a nonstick skillet. Add chicken and sauté over medium-high heat until browned on both sides, about 10 minutes. Transfer to a broiler pan. Divide pesto among chicken breasts, spreading almost to the edge. Top with cheese slices and grill just until the cheese has melted.

Roast Turkey

SERVES 8

12-pound fresh turkey

2 lemons, halved

1 large bunch fresh thyme, 6 to 8 sprigs

¼ cup (½ stick) butter, melted

Preheat the oven to 350°F. Remove the giblets and rinse turkey inside and out. Remove any excess fat and leftover feathers and pat dry. Place turkey in a large roasting pan. Liberally salt and pepper the cavity of the turkey, then stuff with lemons and thyme. Brush the outside of the turkey with the butter and sprinkle with salt and pepper. Tie the legs together with string and tuck the wing tips under the body of the turkey. Roast for 2½ hours, basting occasionally with pan juices, until the juices run clear when you cut between the leg and the thigh. Remove the turkey to a carving board and cover with foil; let it rest for 20 minutes. Slice the turkey and serve hot.

Southern Fried Chicken

SERVES 4

Words cannot describe . . . SENSATIONAL!

8 chicken pieces

2 cups buttermilk

4 cups peanut oil

2 cups Spicy Seasoned
   Flour (page 137)

Place chicken pieces in a bowl and cover with buttermilk. Cover and refrigerate for at least 4 hours or overnight. Remove chicken from buttermilk, shaking off the excess. Toss in seasoned flour. Then repeat: Doing this twice will result in a yummy, crispier coating. Preheat the oven to 350°F. Heat oil in a deep-fryer (or in a deep saucepan). When hot, add 3 chicken pieces at a time and cook for 6 to 8 minutes, or until a nice rich, golden brown. Place on a wire rack set on a baking sheet. When all chicken is fried, place in the oven and bake for 10 minutes, or until cooked through.

TIP: Soaking in buttermilk first creates a really lovely, silky flavor and texture.

Spicy Seasoned Flour

MAKES 2 CUPS

2 cups all-purpose flour

1 teaspoon dried red pepper flakes

2½ teaspoons Chinese five-spice powder

Combine flour, red pepper flakes, five-spice powder, and salt and pepper to taste. Store in an airtight container until needed. This is a sensational coating for frying chicken, duck, fish, or just about anything . . . *Yummo!*

Sweet & Spicy Chicken

SERVES 3

½ cup orange marmalade

1 to 2 teaspoons chili powder

6 chicken drumsticks

Preheat the oven to 350°F. Combine marmalade and chili powder in a plastic bag, add chicken, and shake until evenly coated. Place chicken in a baking dish and spoon over any remaining marmalade mix. Bake for 40 to 50 minutes, or until cooked through.

TIP: To determine when your drumsticks are done, if you pierce them with a fork and the juices run clear, not red-tinged, they are done.

Tomato-Flavored Chicken Legs

SERVES 4 TO 6

A recipe from Verna Day.

2 pounds chicken drumsticks

1 can (10.75 ounces) condensed tomato soup

1 envelope French onion soup mix

Preheat the oven to 350°F. Place the chicken in a baking dish. Combine tomato soup, onion soup mix, and ⅓ cup water and pour over chicken. Bake for 1 hour.

Zingy Chicken

SERVES 4

1 egg, beaten

¼ cup soy sauce

1½ pounds skinless, boneless chicken breast halves, cut into thickish slices

1 cup crushed cornflakes

Preheat the oven to 350°F. Combine egg and soy sauce and dip chicken slices into it. Coat with crushed cornflakes. Place on a baking sheet and bake for 20 to 30 minutes.

FISH & SHELLFISH

Great love and great achievements involve great risks!
—Anonymous

Baked Lemon Fish
SERVES 2

2 white fish fillets
 (5 to 6 ounces each)

1 teaspoon butter, melted

1 lemon, thinly sliced

Preheat the oven to 350°F. Coat fish with butter and season with salt and pepper. Lay lemon over fish. Wrap fish fillets individually in foil. Bake for 20 minutes, or until fish is tender.

Baked Salmon with Pesto Crust
SERVES 4

THIS IS FANTASTIC!

4 salmon steaks
 (5 ounces each)

½ cup pesto

½ cup finely grated
 pecorino cheese

1 lemon

Preheat the oven to 350°F. In a large skillet, sear salmon steaks on each side for 2 minutes. Meanwhile, combine pesto and cheese. Spread over salmon steaks and squeeze fresh lemon juice over the top. Bake for 15 minutes.

Beer Batter for Fish

MAKES 2 CUPS

A recipe from Rach's brother, Anthony "Spud" Moore.

2 egg whites

1 cup all-purpose flour

1 cup beer

Whisk egg whites until light and fluffy. Place flour and a pinch of sea salt in a bowl, then mix in beer until smooth and lump free. Fold in egg whites and allow to stand for 10 to 15 minutes before using.

Blackened Fish

SERVES 4

⅓ cup lime juice

3 tablespoons olive oil

1 tablespoon Cajun spice blend

4 white fish fillets (6 ounces each)

In a shallow dish, combine lime juice, 2 tablespoons oil, Cajun spice, and salt and pepper to taste. Add fish, coat well, and let stand for 10 minutes. Preheat a large nonstick skillet over high heat and add remaining tablespoon oil. Remove fish from marinade and cook for 3 minutes per side, or until cooked through.

OPTIONAL: This is lovely with White Bean Puree (page 105).

Caesar's Fish

SERVES 2

2 white fish fillets (4 to 5 ounces each)

½ cup Caesar salad dressing

1 cup crushed cornflakes

½ cup shredded Cheddar cheese

Preheat the oven to 325°F. Arrange fillets in a single layer in a baking dish. Drizzle fillets with dressing. Sprinkle cornflakes and then cheese over the top. Bake for 10 to 15 minutes, or until fish flakes easily with a fork.

Citrus-Glazed Salmon

SERVES 2

⅓ cup packed dark brown sugar

Grated zest of 1 lemon

2 salmon steaks (5 ounces each)

Preheat the broiler, with the rack 3 inches from the heat. Mix sugar with the zest and add 1½ teaspoons salt and ½ teaspoon pepper. Line a baking sheet with nonstick foil (nonstick side up). Place salmon on foil and spread with brown sugar glaze. Broil salmon for 6 to 8 minutes, or until the thickest part of the salmon reaches an internal temperature of 130°F. Let stand for 5 minutes before serving.

OPTIONAL: This is especially nice with couscous, rice, or salad.

Creamy Basil Fish

SERVES 4

4 white fish fillets (4 ounces each)

¼ cup sour cream

1 tablespoon lemon juice

3 tablespoons finely chopped fresh basil leaves

Preheat the broiler. Place fish on a broiler pan and broil for 3 minutes on each side, until cooked. In a small saucepan, combine sour cream, lemon juice, and basil and heat slowly; do not boil. Serve over fish.

OPTIONAL: This is *magic* served with Sautéed Lemon Potatoes (page 89) and a fresh green salad.

Crispy Fish

SERVES 4

1 cup buttermilk

2¼ pounds thick white fish fillets, cut into ¾-inch strips

½ cup fine cornmeal or all-purpose flour

4 cups peanut oil

Pour buttermilk into a bowl, add fish strips, and soak for 1 hour. In a shallow bowl, season cornmeal with salt and pepper. Shake excess liquid off fish and roll the fish in the seasoned cornmeal. Heat oil to 350°F in a deep-fryer or large deep skillet. Fry fish in batches for 2 minutes, until golden brown.

OPTIONAL: Serve with a corn salsa and a crisp, green salad.

Curried Fish with Coconut Rice

SERVES 4

1 can (14 ounces) coconut milk

1 cup jasmine rice

4 white fish fillets (4 ounces each), cut into ¾-inch cubes

1 jar (15 ounces) korma curry cooking sauce

In a saucepan, bring ½ cup water and coconut milk to a boil. Add rice and cook for 12 to 15 minutes, or until rice is tender and liquid has been absorbed. In a separate saucepan, combine fish with curry sauce. Bring to a boil and simmer for 5 minutes, or until fish is cooked. Serve fish mixture over rice.

OPTIONAL: Garnish with cilantro.

Deep-fried Shrimp

SERVES 4

24 large shrimp, peeled (leaving tail) and deveined

2 eggs, beaten

6 ounces panko bread crumbs

1 cup sunflower oil

Dip shrimp in egg. Then coat with panko. In a large pan, bring oil to a high heat and deep-fry shrimp to a golden color, about 2 minutes.

OPTIONAL: Dust the shrimp in all-purpose flour before dipping in egg.

Fish Fillets with Orange Sauce

SERVES 4

1 orange

2 tablespoons dry white wine

3 tablespoons butter, melted

4 white fish fillets (4 ounces each)

Grate zest from orange to get 2 tablespoons. Squeeze orange to get 2 tablespoons juice. In a small bowl, combine orange juice, wine, and 2 tablespoons of the butter. In a heavy skillet, heat remaining 1 tablespoon butter. Add fish to the skillet and pour half of orange-wine mixture on top. Sprinkle with sea salt, pepper, and the orange zest. Cook for 2 minutes, pour remaining orange-wine sauce over fish, and continue cooking until fish is done. Fish should flake easily with a fork.

Fish Pie

SERVES 4

A McCosker household staple—yummy!

1½ cups tomato and basil pasta sauce

1 pound white fish fillets, cut into chunks

6 Yukon Gold potatoes

1 cup grated Cheddar cheese

In a skillet, warm pasta sauce over medium heat. Add fish and cook for 8 minutes, or until fish is done. Remove from heat and pour into a baking dish. Meanwhile, peel the potatoes and cut into chunks. Cook in boiling water until tender. Drain and mash. Preheat the broiler. Spread mashed potatoes over fish mixture and sprinkle with cheese. Broil until cheese has melted and turned a lovely golden color.

OPTIONAL: This is delicious served with some glazed carrots, and peas with a little finely chopped scallion.

Fish with Black Bean Sauce

SERVES 4

¼ cup black bean and garlic sauce

1 tablespoon sesame oil

4 fish steaks

¼ cup sesame seeds

Preheat the broiler. Mix black bean and garlic sauce and sesame oil together. Spread on fish steaks. Sprinkle with sesame seeds and broil for 4 minutes on each side, or until fish is cooked. Baste with sauce when turning.

Fish with Mango and Kiwifruit

SERVES 4

4 white fish fillets (4 ounces each)

2 tablespoons butter, melted

2 kiwifruit, peeled and sliced

1 mango, peeled and sliced

Preheat a broiler or grill. Brush fish with half the butter. Broil or grill for 3 to 5 minutes per side, depending on thickness. Sauté kiwi and mango lightly in the remaining butter. Serve layered on top of fish.

OPTIONAL: Diced kiwifruit and mango team really well with cucumber, lime juice, and hot pepper as a salsa over grilled fish or chicken.

Garlic Cream Shrimp

SERVES 4

A classic from Aine Watkins that'll make anyone a chef!

2 cups rice

1 tablespoon minced garlic

½ cup heavy cream

16 jumbo shrimp, peeled and deveined

Cook rice according to package directions, then rinse under hot water. Meanwhile, place garlic and cream in a wok or nonstick skillet and reduce cream over medium heat by one-quarter. Add shrimp and cook for 3 to 4 minutes, or until they've turned orange in color. Serve on a bed of rice.

Ginger Shrimp

SERVES 4

1 clove garlic, minced

2 teaspoons minced fresh ginger

2 tablespoons lemon juice

1 pound large shrimp, peeled and deveined

In a skillet, cook garlic and ginger in lemon juice for 1 minute. Add shrimp and cook for 3 to 4 minutes, or until they've turned orange. Serve immediately.

Herbed Fillets

SERVES 2

Serve with a fresh garden salad. . . . Yummy!

2 white fish fillets (4 ounces each)

2 tablespoons lemon juice

2 tablespoons chopped flat-leaf parsley

2 tablespoons chopped fresh basil leaves

Preheat the broiler. Baste the fillets with half the lemon juice, then broil for 3 to 4 minutes per side. Sprinkle with herbs and remaining lemon juice, and season to serve.

Lemon Grilled Fish

SERVES 4

4 white fish fillets (4 ounces each)

1 tablespoon lemon-pepper seasoning

1 scallion, finely chopped

Preheat a broiler or grill. Sprinkle fish generously with lemon-pepper seasoning. Cover and refrigerate for 15 minutes. Broil or grill until flesh is white and flakes easily when tested with a fork. Garnish with scallion.

Mustard Shrimp

SERVES 4

Delightfully EASY!

¼ cup (½ stick) butter

24 large shrimp, peeled and deveined

1 cup heavy cream

2 tablespoons Dijon mustard

In a large skillet, melt butter. Add shrimp and cook, stirring frequently, for 3 to 4 minutes. Pour in cream, season with salt and pepper to taste, and stir in mustard. Simmer gently over low heat for 4 minutes.

OPTIONAL: Serve over rice.

Pan-fried Fish

SERVES 4

3 to 4 slices stale bread, finely grated

4 white fish fillets (4 ounces each)

1 egg, beaten

2 tablespoons butter

Season bread crumbs generously with sea salt and pepper. Dip fillets into egg and then into bread crumbs. Heat a large nonstick skillet over medium heat and add butter. Cook the fish for 3 minutes per side, or until cooked to your liking.

TIP: Frozen bread grates easily.

Phyllo Fish

SERVES 4

8 sheets phyllo dough

2 tablespoons butter, melted

4 white fish fillets (4 ounces each)

½ cup ketchup

Preheat the oven to 400°F. Brush a sheet of phyllo dough with some butter and lay a second sheet on top. Place a piece of fish at the bottom of the pastry and season with sea salt and pepper. Spoon 2 tablespoons of ketchup onto the fish and roll, tucking in pastry sides to make a neat, closed parcel. Repeat with the remaining dough. Lay parcels on the baking sheet and brush the top of each with more butter. Bake for 12 minutes, or until golden brown.

TIP: For a nice presentation, cut each parcel on the diagonal to serve.

Quick Mango Fish

SERVES 4

Recipe by Tony Van Dijk.

4 pieces swordfish, mahimahi, or marlin

½ cup olive oil

Cracked pepper

2 mangoes, sliced

Coat fish liberally with oil and cracked pepper. Cook on a medium-hot grill or in a nonstick skillet over medium heat until the flesh turns white halfway through. Grind more cracked pepper onto it and flip to cook second side. Meanwhile, grill or sauté mangoes. Serve with fish.

Salmon & Spinach Phyllo

SERVES 2

¾ to 1 cup frozen spinach, thawed and squeezed dry

4 sheets phyllo dough

2 tablespoons butter, melted

2 salmon steaks (5 ounces each)

Preheat the oven to 350°F. Place spinach in a bowl and season with sea salt and pepper. Place 1 sheet of phyllo on a flat surface and brush with butter; place the other sheet on top. Place a salmon steak in the center of each and top with half the spinach. Brush with butter and fold the pastry to enclose salmon. Repeat with remaining phyllo and salmon. Brush again with butter and place on a baking sheet. Bake for 25 minutes or until golden and cooked.

OPTIONAL: Crush a clove of garlic into the spinach for an enriched flavor. This is nice served with Horseradish, Mustard & Walnut Cream Sauce (page 47).

Sautéed Shrimp & Peppers in Orange Juice

SERVES 6

3 red bell peppers, halved

2 tablespoons olive oil

30 large shrimp, peeled and deveined

Grated zest and juice of 1 orange

Preheat the broiler. Place peppers on a baking sheet and broil until the skin starts to blister. When cool enough to handle, remove the skin and slice the skinned peppers into strips. In a large skillet, heat oil, add pepper strips, season with salt and black pepper, and sauté for 2 minutes. Add shrimp and cook, stirring occasionally, for 4 minutes. Pour in orange zest and juice and simmer for 2 to 3 minutes, or until the shrimp are cooked through. Taste and adjust the seasoning to serve.

Shrimp & Okra Gumbo

SERVES 4

3 slices bacon, chopped

½ pound fresh okra, cut into quarters

1 can (14.5 ounces) diced tomatoes with onion and garlic

8 extra-jumbo shrimp, peeled and deveined

In a large skillet, sauté bacon until browned. Add okra and tomatoes. Cook over low heat until okra is just tender. Add shrimp and continue to cook until they are cooked through. Season to taste.

OPTIONAL: Serve with rice or crusty corn bread to soak up the delicious juices.

LAMB

Asian-Style Lamb Chops
SERVES 4

8 lamb rib chops

⅓ cup dry sherry

⅓ cup soy sauce

Preheat the broiler. Trim fat from chops. Marinate chops in sherry and soy sauce for 10 minutes. Drain and reserve marinade. Broil chops, turning and brushing with marinade, until done to your liking.

Lamb Pesto Chops
SERVES 3

Everyone looooooooooooooooves these!

6 lamb rib chops

3 tablespoons pesto

3 tablespoons grated Parmesan cheese

Preheat the broiler. Over high heat in a nonstick skillet, cook the chops for 3 minutes per side, or until done to your liking. Remove from heat and place on broiler pan. Combine pesto and Parmesan; place 1 tablespoon of mixture on top of each chop. Grill for 3 to 4 minutes, or until the topping is golden brown.

Lamb Shank Casserole

SERVES 4

4 lamb shanks

1 large onion, coarsely chopped

1 envelope French onion soup mix

1 teaspoon Worcestershire sauce

Place lamb shanks and onion in a large saucepan. Mix soup and Worcestershire sauce with 3 cups water and pour over shanks. Cover and cook on low heat for 4 hours.

OPTIONAL: Serve over mashed potatoes. Add 2 tablespoons of tomato sauce to casserole for extra flavor.

Roast Lamb

SERVES 4 TO 6

A recipe by Jan Neale (and one we love to be invited to on a Sunday night). Serve with roast vegetables and gravy.

2¼ pounds leg (or shoulder) of lamb

1 sprig rosemary

2 cloves garlic, sliced

2 tablespoons olive oil

Preheat the oven to 400°F. With a sharp knife, make ¾-inch slits in the lamb in several places and insert 6 rosemary leaves and a slice of garlic into each. Coat the lamb with oil, place it in a roasting pan, and roast for about 1 hour.

Tandoori Lamb

SERVES 4

A recipe from our treasured Anthony "Spud" Moore. Mmmmm!

8 lamb rib chops

1 cup tandoori paste

1 cup plain yogurt

¼ cup chopped cilantro

Trim fat from chops. Mix ½ cup of tandoori paste, ½ cup yogurt, and 2 tablespoons cilantro and coat lamb. Let stand in a covered bowl for 1 hour in the fridge. In a large nonstick skillet, pan-fry chops for 4 to 5 minutes per side until done. Spoon remaining yogurt and tandoori over the tops of the cooking chops. Sprinkle with the remaining cilantro to serve.

Tangy Lamb Balls

SERVES 4

A recipe worth trying from Perditta O'Connor!

1 pound ground lamb

1 teaspoon curry powder

3 tablespoons Thai sweet chili sauce

1 tablespoon zest and juice of 1 lemon

Combine all ingredients in a large bowl. Roll into balls. In a nonstick skillet, cook until crispy on the outside and cooked on the inside.

OPTIONAL: Mince a clove of garlic and add to the mixture.

PASTA

"Al dente," which is used to describe pasta that is cooked to perfection, in Italian literally means "to the tooth." Pasta that is al dente should not be overly firm, nor should it be overly soft. . . . Good luck!!!

AB's Pasta

SERVES 4

A recipe by Allistair Beattie that amazed us with its simplicity and taste!

12 ounces spaghetti

4 slices bacon, diced

¼ cup sun-dried tomato pesto, or more to taste

½ cup pine nuts, toasted

Cook the spaghetti according to package directions. Meanwhile, cook the bacon until crisp. Drain spaghetti and toss with pesto, bacon, and pine nuts. Add more pesto, if desired.

Blue Broccoli Fusilli Pasta

SERVES 4

1 pound fusilli

1 large stalk broccoli, cut into florets

4½ ounces blue cheese

1¼ cups crème fraîche

Cook pasta according to package directions. Meanwhile, cook broccoli in a saucepan of boiling water for 5 minutes, or until just cooked through, then drain. Put blue cheese and crème fraîche in a large skillet over low heat and reduce to a thick, creamy sauce. Season with pepper. Toss with broccoli and pasta, heat through, and serve warm.

OPTIONAL: Served topped with toasted pine nuts.

Florentine Carbonara

SERVES 4

Recipe from Julie Stephens. THIS IS TIMELESS!!

12 ounces spaghetti

5 slices bacon, diced

2 eggs, lightly beaten

1½ cups grated Parmesan cheese

Cook pasta according to package directions. Meanwhile, in a skillet, cook bacon until crisp. Drain pasta, add beaten eggs, and toss together thoroughly. Add bacon and most of the Parmesan, and mix together. Serve sprinkled with remaining Parmesan.

OPTIONAL: Fry bacon with a little garlic.

Garden Penne Pasta

SERVES 4

2 cups penne pasta

1 cup chopped fresh basil

5 tomatoes, diced

¼ cup extra-virgin olive oil

Cook pasta according to package directions. Drain and add the remaining ingredients, tossing lightly to combine. Season and serve.

Meg's Pasta

SERVES 2

A recipe by Meg Wilson of Houston, Texas.

8 ounces pasta

4 ounces prosciutto, shredded

1 avocado, cubed

3 tablespoons chili oil

Cook pasta according to package directions. Drain, add remaining ingredients, toss, and serve.

OPTIONAL: Prosciutto can be replaced by 4 ounces of cooked shrimp.

Pasta with Crab & Lemon Cream Sauce

SERVES 4

A recipe from Kirsty Morrison of Los Angeles, California.
. . . Yummmmmmmmmmmmmm!!

1 pound spiral pasta

1¼ cups heavy cream

Grated zest of 1 lemon

¾ pound fresh crabmeat

Cook pasta according to package directions. Meanwhile, in a medium saucepan, combine cream and zest and bring to a boil. Add crabmeat and stir gently until heated through. Remove from heat and pour over drained pasta.

OPTIONAL: This is really nice with ¼ cup chopped flat-leaf parsley mixed in.

PORK

Think P.I.G.—that's my motto. P stands for persistence, I stands for integrity, and G stands for guts. These are all the ingredients for a successful life.

—Linda Chandler

American-Style Pork Ribs

SERVES 4

1¼ cups steak sauce

1 tablespoon white wine vinegar

1½ teaspoons smoked paprika

5½ pounds baby back ribs

Combine steak sauce, vinegar, and smoked paprika in a large roasting pan with ¼ cup water. Add ribs and turn to coat well. Cover and refrigerate for at least 2 hours, turning occasionally. Preheat the oven to 400°F. Remove ribs from marinade and reserve marinade. Place ribs on wire racks on 2 foil-lined baking sheets. Bake for 40 minutes, or until well browned, brushing every 10 minutes with reserved marinade.

Apricot & Mustard Pork Chops

SERVES 4

Kim's father-in-law loves these!

⅓ cup apricot jam

2 tablespoons Dijon mustard

4 pork loin chops

3 scallions, finely chopped

Preheat the broiler. In a small saucepan, cook and stir apricot jam and mustard over low heat until jam is melted. Set aside. Broil pork chops for 3 minutes on each side. Brush with half the glaze and broil for another 3 minutes per side. Brush with the remaining glaze and broil for 2 to 4 minutes longer, or until meat juices run clear. Top with scallions to serve.

Bourbon & Brown Sugar Pork Tenderloin

SERVES 6

This is a great dinner party main.

¼ cup soy sauce

¼ cup bourbon

2 tablespoons brown sugar

1¼ pounds pork tenderloin

Mix soy sauce, bourbon, and sugar. Marinate pork in the mixture for 2 to 3 hours in the fridge, basting occasionally. Preheat the oven to 300°F. Place pork in a baking dish and bake for 1 hour, basting occasionally. Slice to serve.

Fried Sausages

SERVES 4

8 pork sausages
  (1¼ pounds total)
2 tablespoons all-purpose
  flour
¼ cup olive oil

Prick sausages with a fork. Season flour with sea salt and pepper. Roll sausages in seasoned flour. In a nonstick skillet, heat oil over medium heat. Add sausages and gently fry, turning every 5 minutes, for 15 to 20 minutes, or until browned.

OPTIONAL: Serve with gravy and mashed potatoes.

Ham on the Bone

SERVES 8

A fabulous Christmas centerpiece by Kendra Horwood.

½ ham on the bone
30 whole cloves
⅔ cup bottled ham glaze or
  marmalade
24 fresh, plump cherries

Preheat the oven to 325°F. Remove outer skin of ham and reserve (use when storing ham to keep moist). Using a sharp knife, score the fat into diamond shapes. Place ham on a rack in a roasting pan, push cloves into the corners of each diamond, and brush fat with glaze. Pour 1½ cups water into the roasting pan. Bake ham for 20 to 25 minutes, or until golden, then remove from the oven and set aside. If there is liquid in the bottom of the pan, place pan on the stove and reduce over medium heat until syrupy. Pour over ham before serving. Garnish the ham with cherries before serving.

Pepperoni Pizzas

MAKES 4

The world's most popular pizza.

1 cup pizza sauce

4 pocketless pita breads or individual-size prebaked pizza crusts

2 cups shredded mozzarella cheese

1 cup sliced pepperoni

Preheat the oven to 400°F. Spread pizza sauce over bread or crusts. Sprinkle with cheese and top with scattered pepperoni. Bake directly on the oven rack for 8 to 10 minutes, or until cheese is melted, bubbling, and beginning to brown. Let cool for 5 minutes before serving.

OPTIONAL: Mix 1 tablespoon of mustard with pizza sauce.

Pork & Bacon Wraps

SERVES 4

D.E.L.I.C.I.O.U.S!

1 pork tenderloin, (about 1 pound)

⅓ cup pesto

4 slices bacon

½ cup applesauce

Preheat the oven to 350°F. Cut pork tenderloin crosswise into 1- to 1½-inch pieces. Spread pieces with two-thirds of pesto. Wrap bacon around pieces to cover outside. Bake for 25 to 30 minutes, or until pork is cooked through. Mix remaining pesto with applesauce and heat until almost boiling. Serve alongside pork.

Pork & Coconut Satay Sticks

SERVES 4

F.a.b.u.l.o.u.s!

¾ cup coconut milk

2 tablespoons chunky peanut butter

2 tablespoons curry powder

1 pound pork, cut for stir-fry

In a bowl, blend coconut milk, peanut butter, curry powder, and sea salt and pepper to taste until smooth. Add pork and marinate overnight in the fridge. Soak bamboo skewers in water before threading with pork. Cook on a hot grill for 10 to 15 minutes, turning constantly so as not to burn. Baste with coconut milk marinade as they cook.

OPTIONAL: Serve with a lovely fresh Mediterranean salad.

Pork Spareribs

SERVES 4

These are SOOOO nice!!

8 pork spareribs

Olive oil spray

1 bottle (12 ounces) honey, soy, and garlic marinade

Boil ribs first for 5 to 10 minutes to remove excess fat. Drain. Place ribs on large foil-lined rimmed baking sheet that has been sprayed with oil. Cover both sides of each rib generously with marinade. Refrigerate for at least 30 minutes before broiling. Broil for 5 minutes on each side, basting with remaining marinade, until juices run clear.

OPTIONAL: Serve with rice and Crunchy Snow Peas (page 97).

Pork Tenderloin Bake

SERVES 6

Quick. Easy. Yummy. Gotta love it!!

1¼ pounds pork tenderloin

1 can (10.75 ounces) condensed tomato soup

1 envelope French onion soup mix

2 tablespoons Worcestershire sauce

Preheat the oven to 300°F. Place tenderloin in a covered baking dish. Combine condensed soup (plus ¼ cup water swished in the can), soup mix, and Worcestershire sauce and pour over meat. Cover and bake for 1 hour. Cut meat into 1-inch slices and use the soup as a gravy.

Rich Tomato Pork

SERVES 4

A really lovely recipe from Tanya Ormsby.

4 pork loin chops

2 cloves garlic, crushed

1 can (14.5 ounces) seasoned diced tomatoes (basil and garlic, or oregano and basil)

½ cup cream

In a nonstick skillet over high heat, cook pork chops for 2 minutes on each side, or until golden. Reduce heat, add garlic and tomatoes, and season to taste. Bring to a boil, then reduce heat to a simmer and cook for 20 minutes. Just before serving, add cream and turn up the heat to thicken the yummy sauce.

OPTIONAL: Serve with mashed potatoes and Beans with Garlic and Pine Nuts (page 94).

Roast Pork

SERVES 8

From Lisa Darr. This continues to stand the test of time— a classic always does!

2¼ pounds boneless fresh ham

3 tablespoons olive oil

Preheat the oven to 425°F. Place ham in a small roasting pan. Rub 1 tablespoon oil onto rind. Grind sea salt over rind and rub into meat. Pour remaining oil into pan and place pan in the oven. Roast for 20 minutes, reduce heat to 350°F, and roast for 1 hour.

OPTIONAL: Serve with roast vegetables, gravy, and applesauce. Kim's husband, Glen, scores the skin, then slathers it with fresh lemon juice and loads of ground sea salt. Makes a *divine crackling*!

Sausage Bake

SERVES 4

So easy, so tasty, so cheap!

6 thick pork sausages (about 3 ounces each)

2 cups chopped vegetables: celery, onion, carrot, broccoli, cauliflower, etc.

½ cup grated Cheddar cheese

1 can (10.75 ounces) condensed cream of mushroom soup

Preheat the oven to 300°F. Combine sausages, chopped vegetables, cheese, and canned soup (along with ¼ cup water swished in the can) and place in a covered baking dish. Season with sea salt and pepper. Cover and bake for 45 minutes. Uncover, stir, and bake 15 minutes longer.

Tangy Pork Chops

SERVES 4

Simply sensational.

4 pork loin chops

½ cup honey

¼ cup Worcestershire sauce

¼ cup ketchup

Lightly broil pork chops until just browned, then place in a shallow baking dish. Combine remaining ingredients and pour over chops. Cover and bake in a preheated 325°F oven for 45 minutes.

Texan Chops

SERVES 4

1 tablespoon olive oil

4 thickish pork chops

1 cup salsa

2 jalapeños, chopped

Rub oil onto pork and season with salt and pepper to taste. Heat a skillet over medium-high heat, add pork, and cook for 4 minutes, or until browned on one side. Flip and cook the other side for 4 minutes, or until done. Reduce the heat, add salsa and jalapeños, and simmer for 20 minutes, or until pork is cooked through.

VEGETARIAN

Girls are like phones: We love to be held and talked to, but if you press the wrong button you'll be disconnected!

—Anonymous

Baked Ravioli

SERVES 4 TO 6

1 container (20 to 28 ounces) fresh ravioli

2½ cups pasta sauce (your favorite)

2 cups grated Parmesan cheese

3 sprigs parsley, chopped

Preheat the oven to 375°F. Cook ravioli for slightly less time than given in package directions. Drain. Set aside ½ cup pasta sauce and 1 cup Parmesan for topping. Line a 9 by 13-inch baking dish with a thin layer of remaining pasta sauce. Add a layer of ravioli and sprinkle a layer of cheese and parsley. Repeat the layering process, finishing with ravioli. Top with reserved pasta sauce and cheese. Sprinkle with parsley and season with salt and pepper. Bake for 15 minutes, or until cheese is melted and bubbling. Cut into squares as you would lasagne.

OPTIONAL: Serve with a big mixed green salad.

Bean Jambalaya

SERVES 4

1 can (15 ounces) red kidney beans, drained

1 can (14.5 ounces) diced tomatoes with peppers and onions

3 cloves garlic, minced

1 teaspoon paprika

Drain beans, place in a saucepan, and add water to cover. Cook beans for 40 minutes, or until tender. Drain and set aside. In another saucepan, combine tomatoes, garlic, and paprika. Bring to a boil, turn down the heat, add beans, and simmer until the sauce thickens. Season to taste with salt and pepper.

OPTIONAL: Serve over rice. Cilantro mixed in at the end or sprinkled on top adds a little green to this dish. Add some black-eyed peas if you like.

Cheesy Cabbage Pasta Bake

SERVES 4

3 cups cooked penne pasta (about 1½ cups uncooked)

1 head Savoy cabbage, shredded

1 cup grated Cheddar cheese

2 slices whole-grain bread, finely grated

Preheat the oven to 350°F. In a baking dish, place alternating layers of pasta, cabbage, two-thirds of the cheese, and salt and pepper to taste. Sprinkle with bread crumbs and remaining cheese and bake for 10 to 15 minutes, or until bubbling.

Eggplant & Sweet Potato Curry

SERVES 4

2 onions, sliced

1 eggplant, peeled and cut into ¾-inch chunks

¾ to 1 pound sweet potatoes, peeled and chopped

1 jar (15 ounces) korma curry cooking sauce

In a skillet, cook onions in ¼ cup simmering water until tender. Drain and set aside. In the same skillet, cook eggplant until browned evenly. Return onions to the skillet and add sweet potato and korma sauce. Fill the empty curry sauce jar halfway with water and add to the skillet. Simmer for 20 to 30 minutes, until the sweet potato and eggplant are tender.

OPTIONAL: Serve with rice and pappadums.

Eggs in Taters

SERVES 4

4 large baking potatoes

¼ cup (½ stick) butter

2 tablespoons cream

4 eggs

Preheat the oven to 400°F. Prick the potatoes with a fork and bake for 1 hour, or until tender. Remove and carefully cut in half. Use a teaspoon to scoop out 90 percent of the flesh, leaving the shells intact. Mash the flesh with the butter and cream and season with salt and pepper. Pile the filling back into the shells and then pop into a baking dish. Make a hollow in the center of each and crack in an egg. Season with salt and pepper. Pop the dish into the oven and bake for 10 to 12 minutes, or until the eggs are just set. Serve hot.

Green Bean Curry

SERVES 4

'Tis easy and yummy.

2 tablespoons Thai red curry paste

6 cups vegetable broth

1 pound green beans, trimmed and halved

1 red bell pepper, diced

In a saucepan, heat curry paste, stirring constantly, for about 1 minute. Add vegetable broth and beans and bring to a rapid boil. Cook for 15 to 20 minutes; halfway through, add bell pepper. Continue to cook until the beans are well done and have absorbed the flavor of the curry broth. Serve over rice.

OPTIONAL: Add canned bamboo shoots or any other veggies you have in the fridge, if desired!

Green Coconut Curry

SERVES 4

Really, really tasty!

4 tablespoons Thai green curry paste

1½ cups cubed sweet potato

1 can (14 ounces) coconut milk

1½ cups (total) cut-up vegetables: broccoli, carrots, zucchini, green beans, etc.

Heat a wok or deep skillet over low heat. Add green curry paste and gently stir-fry for a minute or so. Add sweet potato, coconut milk, and 1 cup water. Bring to a boil, reduce the heat, and gently simmer until sweet potato is almost cooked. Add cut-up vegetables—but not the soft veggies, like zucchini—and simmer for another 10 minutes. When the sweet potato is starting to fall apart, add any soft vegetables. Simmer for another 5 minutes. When all vegetables are cooked and the sweet potato has broken down to almost a puree, the dish is ready.

OPTIONAL: This is delicious served over rice and is nice with chicken, as well.

Mushroom Risotto

SERVES 4

10 ounces mushrooms, chopped

2 cups arborio rice

4 cups vegetable broth

1 cup shaved Parmesan cheese

In a nonstick saucepan, lightly cook mushrooms in 1 tablespoon water to wilt. Add rice and stir until combined. Put broth in another saucepan and bring to a simmer. Stir ⅔ cup broth into the rice. Stir until all the broth is absorbed. Continue adding broth in small quantities, stirring regularly, until absorbed. When this process is finished, add cheese and season with salt and pepper to taste.

OPTIONAL: Add a chopped onion with the mushrooms.

Pasta with Tomato & Basil

SERVES 4

The kids will love this too.

2 cups pasta, any shape

2 cups marinara sauce

½ cup shaved Parmesan cheese

½ cup chopped fresh basil leaves

Cook the pasta according to package directions. Drain. Meanwhile, simmer pasta sauce with ¼ cup of Parmesan. Season to taste. Add the drained pasta and basil, tossing well. Serve sprinkled with remaining Parmesan.

Sour Cream Quiche

SERVES 4 TO 6

1 sheet puff pastry

3 eggs

1¼ cups sour cream

Filling (enough to cover the bottom of the quiche): feta, canned corn, steamed asparagus, baby spinach, sun-dried tomatoes, cooked bacon, sautéed onion, canned tuna, roast chicken

Preheat the oven to 350°F. Line a quiche dish with a round of parchment paper. Fit puff pastry into dish, trimming edges if needed. Beat eggs and sour cream. Add filling of choice to the base. Pour egg mixture on top. Season with sea salt and pepper. Bake for 30 minutes, or until set.

OPTIONAL: Kim's mummy often adds a dollop of ketchup and a drop of Worcestershire sauce to the egg mix for extra flavor.

Spaghetti with Parsley & Parmesan

SERVES 4

1 pound spaghetti

¾ cup (1½ sticks) butter, cut into bits

¼ cup chopped flat-leaf parsley

2 cups grated Parmesan cheese

Cook the pasta according to package directions. Drain and transfer to a warmed serving dish. Add butter, parsley, 1 cup of Parmesan, and salt and pepper to taste. Toss well, using 2 forks, until the butter and cheese have melted. Serve immediately, sprinkled with the remaining cheese.

Vegetable Lasagna

SERVES 6

*Thanks to Kimmy Morrison from New Zealand
for this terrific and very easy dinner!*

2 pounds sweet potato, peeled and sliced

6 sheets no-boil lasagna pasta, rinsed (see Tip)

½ pound Cheddar cheese, grated

2¼ cups pasta sauce, preferably one with vegetables (onion, mushroom, or spinach)

Preheat the oven to 300°F. In a saucepan of boiling water, cook sweet potato until tender. Drain and mash. Line an 8-inch square baking pan with parchment paper. Place 2 sheets of wet lasagna side by side. Spoon one-third of the mashed sweet potato over the pasta and sprinkle with one-third of the cheese. Pour on pasta sauce to cover. Repeat the layering process. Season with salt and pepper. Bake for 35 minutes, or until cheese is slightly golden.

TIP: Always wet no-boil lasagna sheets prior to using, to prevent hard edges.

DESSERTS

Kindness is like sugar: it makes life taste a little sweeter!

—Carla Yerovi

CAKES & COOKIES

A balanced diet is a cookie in each hand.

—Anonymous

Basic Cheesecake

SERVES 8

A classic!

8 ounces cream cheese, softened

1 can (14 ounces) condensed milk

1 envelope gelatin

Cookie Crust (page 180)

In a medium bowl, beat cream cheese until smooth. Add condensed milk and mix until combined. Dissolve gelatin in 3 tablespoons warm water, stirring vigorously until dissolved, then mix into the cream cheese mixture. Pour into the Cookie Crust and chill for at least 4 hours before decorating to serve.

OPTIONAL: Delicious covered with slices of fresh strawberries and kiwifruit or simply a layer of grated chocolate.

Brownies

MAKES 12

These are devilishly delicious!

1 cup Nutella

2 eggs

10 tablespoons all-purpose flour

½ cup chopped hazelnuts

Preheat the oven to 350°F. Line an 8-inch cake pan with parchment paper. Pop the Nutella and eggs into a medium-size bowl and whisk until smooth. Add the flour and whisk until blended. Spoon the batter into the pan and sprinkle with hazelnuts. Bake for 11 to 12 minutes, or until a toothpick inserted in the center comes out with wet, gooey crumbs. Set on a rack to cool completely.

OPTIONAL: Omit the hazelnuts and top with our yummy Peanut Butter Icing (page 186).

Chocolate Slice

SERVES 10

Often slices are mixed in a bowl and baked in a pan—not this one!

13 ounces milk chocolate, broken into pieces

9 tablespoons unsalted butter, melted

10 tablespoons smooth peanut butter

7 ounces graham crackers, crushed

In a microwaveable bowl, melt chocolate, checking every 30 seconds. When melted, stir in butter and peanut butter. Add graham cracker crumbs and mix to combine. Pour into an 8-inch square baking pan and pop into the fridge for 20 minutes to set, then slice (use a hot knife).

Cinnamon Wedges

SERVES 6

10 flour tortillas (10-inch diameter)

½ cup (1 stick) butter, melted

10 tablespoons cinnamon sugar

Preheat the oven to 350°F. Brush both sides of tortillas generously with butter and sprinkle with cinnamon sugar. Cut into wedges and arrange in a single layer on a large baking sheet. Bake for 8 to 10 minutes. (Do this in batches.) Let cool.

OPTIONAL: These are delicious served with Fruit Salsa (page 202) or Kahlúa Dip (page 26).

Coconut Macaroons

MAKES 25 TO 30

Recipe from Lisa Hayes.

2 eggs, separated

¾ cup superfine sugar

3 cups shredded coconut

Preheat the oven to 350°F. Line baking sheets with parchment paper. Add a pinch of salt to egg whites and beat with an electric mixer until soft peaks form. Beat in egg yolks one at a time. Gradually add sugar, beating well after each addition. With a spoon, stir in coconut and mix well. Spoon tablespoons of the mixture onto the baking sheets. Bake for 8 minutes, or until golden brown.

Cookie Crust

7 ounces graham cracker crumbs

5 tablespoons butter, melted

Combine graham cracker crumbs and melted butter. Press mixture into the bottom of a 10-inch springform pan. Chill before using.

OPTIONAL: Add a tablespoon of cinnamon for flavor (and because Oprah said it's good for the brain!).

TIP: One of our Facebook fans told us about a helpful test. Once you have mixed the ingredients together, squeeze a little in your fist; if the mixture holds together, you have the perfect crust.

Cream Cheese Icing

Fabulous over hummingbird and carrot cakes, or dolloped atop muffins and cupcakes.

3 tablespoons cream cheese, softened

1 tablespoon butter, softened

1 teaspoon grated lemon zest (optional)

1½ cups confectioners' sugar

Beat cream cheese and butter together. Add lemon zest (if using) and confectioners' sugar. Continue to beat until the icing is nice and smooth or until you can't resist any longer and lick the spoon!

Easy Pineapple Cake

SERVES 12

A recipe by Brett McCosker. Two words: TRY IT!!!

2 cups self-rising flour

1 cup superfine sugar

2 cans (8 ounces each) crushed pineapple

Preheat the oven to 350°F. Grease a 9-inch springform pan. Pop flour into a mixing bowl and combine with sugar. Add pineapple (juice and all) and mix well. Pour into a 9-inch cake pan and bake for 40 minutes.

Easy Pineapple Cake Icing

MAKES ABOUT 2 CUPS

1 can (14 ounces) condensed milk

½ cup (1 stick) butter, melted

1 cup shredded coconut

½ teaspoon vanilla extract

In a saucepan, combine condensed milk and melted butter and bring to a boil. Stirring constantly, boil for 4 minutes. Add coconut and vanilla and mix. While mixture is hot, spread over cooled cake.

TIP: The above amount covers the entire cake, top and sides. If, however, you want to cover just the top, halve the ingredients.

Flourless Chocolate Cake

SERVES 12

Can be served warm or cold and is delicious with fresh whipped cream.

4 eggs

1 cup superfine sugar

1 stick plus 6 tablespoons butter

9 ounces good-quality dark chocolate

Preheat the oven to 350°F. Line a 9-inch springform pan with parchment paper. Separate eggs. Add ½ cup of the sugar to the yolks and beat well with a mixer. Beat egg whites until fluffy and gradually add remaining ½ cup sugar, beating until stiff peaks form. Melt butter and chocolate over hot water, stirring regularly. Pour into egg yolk mixture and fold. Once combined, fold in egg whites. Scrape batter into cake pan and bake in the lower third of the oven for 40 minutes. Note: This cake will collapse, as it has no flour to sustain the rise.

Fruit Cake

SERVES 8 TO 12

Recipe from Jen Whittington. Delicious and nutritious!
This is B.R.I.L.L.I.A.N.T!

2¼ pounds mixed dried fruits

2 cups fruit juice or cold organic tea of choice

2 tablespoons sherry

2 cups self-rising flour

Soak fruits in juice or tea and sherry overnight. Preheat the oven to 250°F. Line a 9-inch springform pan with parchment paper. Stir flour into soaked fruit and mix well. Spoon into springform pan. Bake for 2½ hours in the bottom third of the oven. Remove pan from oven and let cake cool in the pan. Put into a container or wrap in foil. Keep for 2 to 3 days before cutting.

OPTIONAL: Instead of sherry we have used Cointreau and Grand Marnier . . . mmm! Or delete sherry if you'd prefer the cake nonalcoholic.

Fruit Mince Palmiers

MAKES 16

2 tablespoons superfine sugar

1 sheet puff pastry

½ cup mincemeat

Line a baking sheet with parchment paper and sprinkle sugar over it. Lay pastry on the baking sheet and spread entire surface with mince. Roll up one side tightly until you reach the middle, then repeat with the other side. Freeze for 30 minutes. Preheat the oven to 400°F. Cut the pastry crosswise into ½-inch-thick slices. Lay the slices flat and bake for 15 to 20 minutes or until golden brown.

Kisses

MAKES 20

½ cup (1 stick) butter, plus 1 teaspoon for the pan

1 tablespoon confectioners' sugar

1 tablespoon arrowroot

1 cup self-rising flour

Preheat the oven to 300°F. Cream ½ cup butter and sugar and add arrowroot and flour. Butter a baking sheet with 1 teaspoon butter. For each kiss, scoop a teaspoon of dough onto the sheet and press with a fork. Bake kisses for 8 to 10 minutes, or until pale brown.

OPTIONAL: Join 2 kisses together with some icing or jam when cold.

Meringues

MAKES 12

2 egg whites

½ cup superfine sugar

¼ teaspoon vanilla extract

Preheat the oven to 300°F. Line a baking sheet with parchment paper. Whip egg whites with an electric beater until stiff, then gradually add sugar and vanilla, continuing to beat. Put tablespoonfuls onto the baking sheet. Bake for 20 minutes, or until dry and firm.

TIP: If egg whites are allowed to stand overnight, they will whip up faster. A pinch of salt in egg whites makes them stiffen quickly.

Orange & Almond Cake

SERVES 8 TO 10

A sensational recipe from Fiona Burt.

3 oranges

1 cup superfine sugar

6 eggs

2 cups almond meal

In a saucepan, cover unpeeled oranges with water, bring to a boil, then simmer for 1 hour. Let cool completely, cut in half, remove seeds, and puree. Preheat the oven to 325°F. Grease a cake pan. Beat sugar and eggs together. Add orange puree and almond meal. Stir well, pour into a 9-inch square cake pan, and bake for 70 minutes.

OPTIONAL: Frost with Cream Cheese Icing (page 180).

Peanut Butter Cookies

MAKES AROUND 20

Kids absolutely love 'em.

1 cup chunky peanut butter

1 cup packed brown sugar

1 teaspoon ground cinnamon

1 egg

Preheat the oven to 350°F. Line 2 baking sheets with parchment paper. Mix all ingredients in a bowl. Spoon small tablespoon-size balls onto the baking sheets. Slightly flatten each ball with a fork, crisscross style. Bake for 8 minutes, or until a thin crust forms on the cookie.

OPTIONAL: These are the right texture when they roll without sticking to the palm of your hand.

Peanut Butter Icing

MAKES 3 CUPS

2 cups chunky peanut butter

1½ cups confectioners' sugar

1 tablespoon vanilla extract

2 to 3 tablespoons milk

Stir peanut butter and confectioners' sugar together. Add the vanilla extract and enough milk to make the icing spreadable.

Shortbread

SERVES 8

A recipe by the lovely Jennette McCosker.

½ cup (1 stick) butter

½ cup all-purpose flour

3 tablespoons cornstarch

3 tablespoons confectioners' sugar

Preheat the oven to 350°F. Line an 8-inch square baking pan with parchment paper. Mix all ingredients together in a blender. Press dough into baking pan and bake for 30 minutes.

OPTIONAL: Sprinkle with superfine sugar before baking.

White Chocolate Icing

MAKES ABOUT 1 CUP

This is yummy dolloped on muffins or cakes.

5 ounces white chocolate

½ cup sour cream

In a microwave, melt chocolate, stirring every 30 seconds until nice and smooth. Allow to cool slightly and mix in sour cream.

PIES & PASTRIES

Life is uncertain. Eat dessert first.
—Ernestine Ulmer

Apple Crumble

SERVES 4

A golden oldie—this is really easy and really tasty!

1 can (21 ounces) apple pie filling

½ cup packed brown sugar

½ cup (1 stick) butter, softened

¾ cup all-purpose flour

Preheat the oven to 400°F. Place apple filling in an 8-inch square baking dish. Sprinkle with 2 tablespoons brown sugar. In a bowl, blend butter, flour, and remaining 2 tablespoons brown sugar until crumbly. Sprinkle over apple. Bake for 30 minutes, or until the crumble is golden brown.

OPTIONAL: Add ½ teaspoon ground cinnamon to the apple mix. Serve with custard or ice cream.

Apricot Turnovers

MAKES 4

A recipe from Katherine Knight.

1 sheet puff pastry

4 fresh apricots, sliced

4 tablespoons apricot jam

2 tablespoons confectioners' sugar

Preheat the oven to 350°F. Place puff pastry on a baking sheet and quarter. Cut apricots and evenly place them and the jam in the middle of the 4 quarters. Fold each quarter to form a triangle, pressing with a fork to seal all edges. Make small diagonal cuts across the top of the pastry. Bake for 20 minutes, or until golden brown. Cool, then dust with confectioners' sugar to serve.

Blueberry Puffs

MAKES 4

2 sheets puff pastry

8 ounces blueberries

1 cup superfine sugar

¼ cup butter (½ stick), melted

Preheat the oven to 350°F. Line a baking sheet with parchment paper. Cut pastry in half to make 4 long pieces. Toss blueberries with ¾ cup of the sugar. Place blueberries in the center of pastry pieces, roll up, and brush with butter. Make a few fine cuts on the top and sprinkle with remaining sugar. Place on baking sheet and bake for 15 to 20 minutes, or until golden brown.

OPTIONAL: Serve warm with a scoop of vanilla ice cream.

Caramel Tart

SERVES 6

Recipe from Rachael's great-grandma "Chrissie."
As easy as 1, 2, 3, 4!

1 teaspoon butter

1 refrigerated 9-inch piecrust

1 can (14.1 ounces)
dulce de leche

1 cup heavy cream,
whipped

Preheat the oven to 350°F. Grease a pie plate with butter and line with piecrust. Bake for 8 to 10 minutes, or until golden brown. Set crust aside to cool slightly. Pour dulce de leche into crust. Spoon whipped cream over the dulce de leche.

Cherry Cobbler

SERVES 8

1 can (14 ounces) pitted
sweet cherries, drained

1 package vanilla cake mix

7 tablespoons butter, melted

3½ ounces slivered almonds

Preheat the oven to 350°F. Spread the cherries over the bottom of a loaf pan. Sprinkle cake mix over them, then pour the butter evenly over the cake mix. Sprinkle with almonds and bake for 40 minutes, or until golden brown. Let cool slightly before serving.

OPTIONAL: Serve with whipped cream or ice cream.

Crostoli

MAKES 18

A recipe from Jan Neale—"Nin."
These are delicious served with coffee.

¼ cup superfine sugar

2 tablespoons ground cinnamon

1 refrigerated 9-inch piecrust

1 cup sunflower oil

In a small bowl, combine sugar and cinnamon. Set aside. Cut pastry into ½-inch-wide strips. Twist each strip and place it on a baking sheet. Freeze for 10 to 15 minutes. In a small skillet, heat oil to very hot (350° to 375°F, or when a piece of pastry sizzles in it). Quickly deep-fry the twists in batches, turning once, until golden. Remove and place on paper towels. While still hot, sprinkle with sugar-cinnamon mix.

OPTIONAL: Dust with confectioners' sugar for serving.

Easy Pecan Pie

SERVES 6

This is really easy and really nice!

3 egg whites

1 cup superfine sugar

1 cup pecans, chopped

22 Ritz crackers, crushed

Preheat the oven to 350°F. Beat egg whites until stiff, gently adding the sugar. Fold in pecans and crushed crackers. Pour mixture into a pie plate and bake for 25 minutes.

OPTIONAL: Add a dash of vanilla extract to the Ritz crackers. Slice and top with a dollop of whipped cream and a piece of seasonal fruit.

Jam Tarts

MAKES 10

1 refrigerated 9-inch piecrust

1 tablespoon butter, for the pan

Your choice of jam

1 cup heavy cream, whipped

Preheat the oven to 350°F. Cut as many rounds as possible out of the dough and press the rounds into the cups of a lightly buttered tartlet pan. Press a fork down around the edges for decoration. Bake for 10 minutes. Spoon the desired amount of jam into each tart and return to the oven for another 5 minutes. Let cool to set, and serve with a dollop of whipped cream.

Key Lime Pie

SERVES 8

This is DELECTABLE!!

Cookie Crust (page 180)

4 limes

4 egg yolks

1 can (14 ounces) condensed milk

Preheat the oven to 300°F. Press the Cookie Crust mixture into the bottom and up the sides of a 10-inch pie plate. Grate the zest of 1 lime and juice all 4. With an electric mixer, beat egg yolks until thick and light yellow; don't overmix. Turn the mixer off and mix in the condensed milk by hand. Turn the speed to low and mix in half of the lime juice. Once the juice is incorporated, add the other half and the zest and mix until blended (just a few seconds). Pour the mixture into the cookie crust and bake for 12 minutes to set.

OPTIONAL: Serve with whipped cream.

Ultimate Caramel Macadamia Tart

MAKES 4

The absolute favorite of Rach's dad, Billy Moore.

1 refrigerated 9-inch piecrust

4 ounces semisweet chocolate

1 can (14.1 ounces) dulce de leche

18 macadamia nuts, toasted and chopped

Preheat the oven to 350°F. Cut piecrust into 4 squares and mold into a nonstick muffin tin. Bake for 6 minutes, or until light golden brown. Melt chocolate and brush the insides of the pastry shells. Spoon the dulce de leche into the shells and top with macadamia nuts.

ICE CREAM, MOUSSES & FONDUES

I doubt the world holds for anyone a more soul-stirring surprise than the first adventure with ice cream.

—Heywood C. Broun

Blue Chockie Mousse

SERVES 4

This is berry, berry nice!

8 ounces blueberries

7 ounces dark chocolate

1¼ cups heavy cream

Divide blueberries among four 6- to 8-ounce parfait glasses. Melt chocolate carefully in a bowl in the microwave, stirring every 15 seconds. Remove and allow to cool. Beat cream until soft peaks form, then fold in the melted chocolate. Spoon the mixture over the blueberries and serve immediately.

Choc-Coconut Cream Fondue

SERVES 6

1 can (15 ounces) cream of coconut

2 tablespoons rum

12 ounces semisweet chocolate chips

2 pints strawberries

In a saucepan, combine coconut, rum, and chocolate chips and stir over medium heat until chocolate melts. Pour the mixture into a warm serving bowl and serve with strawberries for dipping.

OPTIONAL: Serve with any fresh fruit. Try banana, pineapple, or mango.

Chocolate Mousse

SERVES 4

This is dreamy.

3½ ounces good-quality dark chocolate

1 tablespoon butter

2 eggs, separated

½ cup heavy cream, whipped

Melt chocolate with butter carefully in a bowl in the microwave, stirring every 15 seconds until smooth. Remove and let cool for a few minutes, then stir in beaten egg yolks and whipped cream. Beat egg whites until soft peaks form, then gently fold into chocolate mixture. Spoon mixture into small dishes or glasses and refrigerate for 3 hours, or until firm.

OPTIONAL: If entertaining, drizzle 1 teaspoon of Grand Marnier, cognac, or rum over each mousse. Serve with extra whipped cream and fresh raspberries and strawberries, dusted with confectioners' sugar.

Citrus Granita

SERVES 4

6 oranges

1½ lemons

¾ cup sugar

Fresh mint sprigs, for garnish

Slice thin strips of zest from the oranges and lemons and set zest aside. Squeeze the juice from the fruit. In a heavy-bottomed saucepan, combine the sugar and 2 cups water, bring to a boil, and stir until the sugar dissolves. Continue to boil for 10 minutes, or until syrupy. Remove from the heat, stir in some of the citrus zest, cover, and let cool. Mix in juice and pour into a freezerproof container. Freeze, uncovered, for 4 hours. Remove and break up with a fork. Freeze again for an additional 4 hours, or until hard. Remove from the freezer and leave until slightly softened. Scrape into glasses and decorate with sprigs of fresh mint and remaining strips of zest.

Cookies & Cream Ice Cream

SERVES 8

Serves not enough!

2½ cups heavy cream, chilled

1 can (14 ounces) condensed milk

1 teaspoon vanilla extract

5 ounces Oreo cookies, roughly crushed

Pour cream into a bowl and beat until *just* thickened. Add condensed milk and vanilla and stir thoroughly. Sprinkle in cookies and gently toss to combine. Pour into a freezerproof container. Freeze for at least 4 hours or overnight.

Ice Cream with a Twist

SERVES 2

2 scoops vanilla ice cream

1 pint strawberries, washed and hulled

2 tablespoons caramelized balsamic vinegar

Place 1 scoop of ice cream in each of 2 bowls. Slice the strawberries and mix with the balsamic vinegar. Once combined, pour over ice cream and serve.

Praline Fondue

SERVES 4 TO 6

Serve with fresh fruit and marshmallows for dipping.

½ cup superfine sugar

¾ cup roasted unsalted almonds

2 cups heavy cream

2 tablespoons cornstarch

Put sugar in a small saucepan, place over low heat, and heat until sugar is melted and golden brown. Stir in almonds and quickly spoon mixture onto a parchment-lined baking sheet. Allow to cool completely before grinding. In a food processor, finely grind the praline mixture and set aside. In a fondue pot or heavy saucepan, stir cream and cornstarch together over medium-high heat until nice and smooth and thick. Stir in the yummy praline powder.

OPTIONAL: Add a dash of vanilla to sugar to taste.

Soft-Serve Frozen Fruit Yogurt

SERVES 4 TO 6

A recipe from Cyndi O'Meara.

2 cups coarsely chopped fruit: bananas, strawberries, mango, blueberries, etc.

½ cup honey

2 cups plain yogurt

Process fruit in a blender until smooth. Add honey and yogurt and mix thoroughly. Pour into a covered container and freeze. Remove from the freezer 20 to 30 minutes before serving.

FRUIT & CANDY

It's different in Europe, because forty is really the best age for a woman.
That's when we hit our peak and become this ripe fruit.

—Juliette Binoche

Barbie Bananas

SERVES 4

A recipe from Tanya Ormsby.

4 bananas

½ cup Baileys Irish Cream (or imitation)

4 scoops ice cream

Preheat a grill. Place the whole bananas on the grill—skins and all! Leave for 4 to 5 minutes, turning once. Slit the top of each and add just enough Baileys to not overflow. Leave for 1 to 2 minutes longer. Remove from the grill and serve with ice cream.

Butterscotch Haystacks

MAKES 36

1⅔ cups (11 ounces) butterscotch baking chips

¾ cup creamy peanut butter

2 cans (5 ounces each) chow mein noodles

3½ cups miniature marshmallows

Line baking sheets with parchment paper. Melt butterscotch chips in a large microwaveable bowl, stirring every 20 seconds until smooth. Stir in peanut butter until well blended. Add chow mein noodles and marshmallows, tossing until all ingredients are coated. Drop by rounded tablespoons onto baking sheets. Refrigerate until ready to serve.

Chocolate Lychees

MAKES 16

A recipe from Meg Wilson.
These are elegant, quick, easy, and amazing with coffee.

4 ounces milk chocolate, chopped

¼ cup heavy cream, at room temperature

16 fresh lychees, peeled, pitted, and patted dry

In a microwaveable dish, melt chocolate in 30-second increments, stirring well after each. Add cream and stir well to combine. Dip lychees to coat. Refrigerate for several minutes to set.

OPTIONAL: If fresh lychees are not in season, canned lychees work just as well.

Chocolate Parcels

MAKES 25

Recipe from Cyndi O'Meara. Y.U.M!

7 ounces semisweet chocolate

1 cup slivered almonds, lightly toasted

½ cup chopped preserved ginger

Line a baking sheet with parchment paper. In a microwaveable dish, melt chocolate in 30-second increments, stirring well after each. Remove from the heat as soon as completely melted. Add almonds and ginger to the melted chocolate and mix well. Spoon small amounts ¾ inch apart on the baking sheet. Refrigerate until hardened. Store in an airtight container in the refrigerator.

Cookie & Cream Truffles

MAKES 40

This recipe R.O.C.K.S!

50 Oreo cookies (about 3 sleeves)

8 ounces cream cheese, softened

1 pound milk or dark chocolate, broken into pieces

4 ounces white chocolate, broken into pieces

In a blender or food processor, crush cookies. Pour into a mixing bowl and add cream cheese, mixing until there are no traces of white. Using a teaspoon, roll the mixture into balls, place on a lined baking sheet, and refrigerate for 45 minutes. Place milk chocolate in a microwaveable container; melt gradually, checking and stirring every 20 seconds until smooth. Coat balls thoroughly with melted chocolate, and put back into the fridge to cool. Melt white chocolate and use a fork to drizzle it over the chocolate truffles to decorate.

Dulce de Leche

MAKES ABOUT 2 CUPS

1 quart whole milk

1½ cups sugar

¼ teaspoon baking soda

1 vanilla bean, split
  (optional)

In a medium heavy-bottomed saucepan, combine milk, sugar, and baking soda. Stir well to dissolve the sugar. Bring to a boil over medium heat without stirring. Remove from the heat and skim off any scum. Add the vanilla bean (if using) and bring to a boil over medium heat. Reduce the heat to very low and simmer gently for 1 hour, stirring frequently. Remove the vanilla bean and discard. Continue to simmer for another 30 minutes to 1 hour over very low heat, stirring frequently, until thick and caramelized. Remove from the heat and let cool.

TIP: Dulce de leche can be stored in a refrigerator in a clean glass jar for 1 to 2 weeks (if it lasts that long!).

Easy Chocolate Fudge

MAKES 20 PIECES

1 can (14 ounces) condensed milk

7 tablespoons butter, cubed

1¼ cups packed brown sugar

7 ounces good-quality dark chocolate, finely chopped

Line an 8-inch square pan with parchment paper. Place all ingredients in a 3-quart microwaveable bowl. Microwave, uncovered, on medium-high in 2-minute increments, stirring after each, for 8 to 10 minutes, or until bubbles appear over the whole surface of the mixture. Pour immediately into the prepared pan. Place in the fridge for 1 hour, or until firm. Cut the fudge into 20 pieces.

OPTIONAL: Add 1 tablespoon corn syrup to the mix before microwaving.

Fruit Salsa

SERVES 6

Sensational.

2 kiwifruit, peeled and diced

2 Golden Delicious apples, peeled and diced

2 pints strawberries, quartered

2 tablespoons sugar

In a large bowl, mix all ingredients. Cover and chill in the refrigerator at least 15 minutes.

OPTIONAL: Serve piled over Cinnamon Wedges (page 179) or spooned over creamy vanilla ice cream.

Gingered Prunes

SERVES 8

By Jocelyn Wilson. These are real treats!!

½ cup heavy cream, whipped

2 ounces crystallized ginger, finely diced

1 tablespoon confectioners' sugar

7 ounces pitted prunes

Combine whipped cream, ginger, and confectioners' sugar. Stuff prunes with the mixture and chill before serving.

Grilled Mango Halves with Lime

SERVES 6

A great barbecue dessert: light and lovely.

3 large mangoes

1 lime

2 tablespoons brown sugar

Cut each mango in half, cutting around the seed and leaving the skin on. Score the skin of each half with a sharp knife, making an X pattern. Squeeze lime juice onto the mango halves. Sprinkle the fruit with the brown sugar. Place the mangoes on a preheated, oiled grill and cook, sugared side down, for 2 to 3 minutes.

OPTIONAL: Serve with a sorbet.

Quick Poached Pears

SERVES 6

A recipe from Wendy Beattie. Simply a sweet success!

6 firm-ripe pears

½ cup white wine

Peel pears and place upright in a microwaveable covered bowl. Pour wine and ⅓ cup water over the pears, cover, and cook on high for 10 minutes, or until soft. Remove and let cool in wine. Once cool, remove pears from wine and serve.

OPTIONAL: This is delicious served drizzled with Easy Mocha Sauce (page 43).

Roasted Honey Pears with Honey Cream

SERVES 4

Your mother-in-law will love it, and you!!!!

3 firm-ripe pears

½ cup honey

2 tablespoons brown sugar

1¼ cups heavy cream, whipped

Preheat the oven to 350°F. Quarter and core pears. Place in a baking dish, drizzle with ¼ cup honey, and sprinkle with brown sugar. Pour ½ cup water around pears. Bake, uncovered, for 30 minutes, or until just soft. Place 3 pear quarters on each of 4 serving plates. Drizzle pan juices over pears. Mix whipped cream and remaining ¼ cup honey together until combined. Serve over pears.

OPTIONAL: Add ¼ teaspoon cinnamon to cream and honey for a lovely flavor.

Rocky Road

SERVES 8

Kim's favorite!!!—A recipe by Jennette McCosker.

9 ounces milk chocolate

1 cup coarsely chopped macadamia nuts

1 cup halved marshmallows

1 cup coarsely chopped Turkish delight candy

Break chocolate into pieces and melt in the microwave on medium-high, stirring every 20 seconds. Allow to cool slightly before adding remaining ingredients. Mix until well combined. Line a rectangular dish with parchment paper, scrape the mixture into it, neaten the edges, and refrigerate until set. Cut into desired serving pieces.

OPTIONAL: Use other nuts—almonds, hazelnuts, Brazil nuts, etc.

Rum Balls

MAKES 15

An absolute treasure from Anthony "Spud" Moore.

1 pound fruitcake

½ cup dark rum

9 ounces dark chocolate

1 cup shredded coconut

Place fruitcake and rum in a food processor and blend until combined. Allow to stand for 30 minutes in the fridge. Melt chocolate. Roll the cake mixture into balls, smother with chocolate, and roll in coconut. Place on a tray and chill before serving.

Toffee Cinnamon Pecans

MAKES 2 CUPS

½ cup (1 stick) butter

1 cup brown sugar

1 teaspoon cinnamon

1 pound pecans

In a microwaveable dish, melt butter. Add brown sugar and cinnamon and cook on high for 3 minutes; remove from the heat, stir, and cook for another minute. Add pecans and cook for 3 to 5 minutes, stirring occasionally so all the pecans are coated. Pour the mixture onto wax paper to cool. When cooled completely, break into pieces and store in an airtight container.

FOR THE CHILDREN

The laughter of a child is the light of a house.

—Anonymous

SAVORY

What is a home without children? Quiet.

—Henny Youngman

Bugs in Rugs

MAKES 12

12 cocktail franks

½ cup ketchup

3 slices whole wheat bread, crusts removed

¼ cup (½ stick) butter, melted

Preheat the oven to 350°F. Pierce franks all over with a fork. Spread ketchup on bread, then cut into quarters. Place a frank diagonally on each quarter of bread. Bring up the edges and secure with a toothpick. Brush liberally with the melted butter. Place on a greased baking sheet and bake for 10 minutes, or until the bread is crisp and light brown. Serve warm.

OPTIONAL: Sprinkle with poppy seeds before baking.

Cheese Bickies

MAKES 12

"Bickies" are crackers Down Under!

1 cup rice flour

3 tablespoons almond meal

1 tablespoon butter

1 cup grated Cheddar cheese

Preheat the oven to 350°F. Combine flour and almond meal and rub in butter. Add cheese. Add a little water, if required, to make into a stiff dough. Roll out on a floured surface and cut into shapes. Bake for 10 to 15 minutes, or until golden.

Easy Pasta

SERVES 4

1 pound lean ground beef

2 cups spaghetti sauce

2 zucchini, sliced

1 package (9 ounces) fresh angel hair pasta

Heat a heavy skillet over medium-high heat. Sauté beef in 3 tablespoons water for 3 to 4 minutes, stirring frequently to break up meat. Stir in spaghetti sauce. Add zucchini and season. Sauté for 2 to 3 minutes longer, and simmer until just heated through. Meanwhile, cook pasta according to package directions. Drain and place on plates topped with prepared sauce.

OPTIONAL: Sprinkle with Parmesan cheese. The kids will love it!

Egg in a Hole

MAKES 1

1 teaspoon butter

1 slice whole wheat bread

1 egg

In a skillet, melt butter. Cut a hole in the bread to fit the egg. Place bread in the skillet and crack egg into the hole. Cook on one side until it just firms, then flip and cook until done.

Fish Cocktails

MAKES 24

Morgan, Jaxson, Hamilton, and Flynn love these!

1 pound white fish fillets

3 tablespoons all-purpose flour

1 egg white

1¼ cups cornflake crumbs

Preheat the oven to 350°F. Line a baking sheet with parchment paper. Cut fish into 1¼-inch cubes. Coat in flour and shake off the excess. Whisk egg white in a small bowl. Dip fish, one piece at a time, in egg white, then coat with cornflake crumbs. Place fish cubes in a single layer on a baking sheet and bake for 15 minutes, or until golden.

Gourmet Baked Beans on Toast

MAKES 4

These are great!

2 teaspoons butter

4 thick slices bread, crust removed

1 can (11 ounces) baked beans

½ cup grated Cheddar cheese

Preheat the oven to 350°F. Butter both sides of bread slices and press into 4 cups of a muffin tin. Bake for 5 to 10 minutes, or until the bread is crisp and golden. Heat the baked beans in a pan over low heat until just warm. Spoon the baked beans into the bread cups and sprinkle with the grated cheese.

Homemade Peanut Butter

MAKES ABOUT 1 CUP

1½ cups unsalted roasted peanuts, skins on

1 to 2 tablespoons peanut oil

In a food processor, combine peanuts and peanut oil. Add a sprinkling of salt. Process the mixture until very smooth. Store in a sealed container in the fridge. It will be good for 2 weeks.

OPTIONAL: For chunky peanut butter, set aside ¼ cup of the peanuts. Process remaining peanuts, oil, and salt as directed. Stir in reserved peanuts and process a few seconds more to create the chunks in your chunky peanut butter.

Mini Hot Dogs

MAKES 8

1 sheet puff pastry

1 egg, beaten

8 cocktail franks

Ketchup, for serving

Preheat the oven to 350°F. Cut pastry into 8 pieces. Brush with beaten egg. Place a frank across each pastry piece and wrap the opposite ends of the pastry around the frank. Brush pastry with egg again. Bake on a baking sheet for 10 to 15 minutes, or until golden. Serve with a bowl of ketchup for dipping.

Mini Pizzas

MAKES 4

Quick and easy! Thanks, Michelle Fredericks.

2 English muffins, split

4 teaspoons pizza sauce

3 slices bacon, cooked until crisp and crumbled

¼ cup shredded mozzarella cheese

Preheat the broiler. Spread muffin halves with pizza sauce. Top with bacon and cheese. Broil until golden brown.

OPTIONAL: Add whatever toppings your "angels" will eat.

Parmesan Twists

MAKES 16

1 sheet puff pastry

¼ cup grated Parmesan cheese

Preheat the oven to 350°F. Line a baking sheet with parchment paper. Cover the puff pastry with Parmesan. Cut in half, and then cut into ¾-inch-wide strips. Twist each strip, place the strips on a baking sheet, and bake for about 5 minutes, or until golden brown. Let cool and store in an airtight container.

OPTIONAL: For added flavor, you can sprinkle the strips with paprika prior to baking.

Sandwich Roll-Ups

MAKES 12

4 slices whole wheat bread

1 tablespoon butter, softened

Sandwich fillings:
    sliced meat or cheese

Bunch of long chives

Remove crusts from bread. Lay slices of bread on a flat surface and, with a rolling pin, roll out until bread is quite thin. Butter lightly and cover each slice with chosen fillings. Roll tightly and cut into thirds. Tie with a chive.

Simple Penne

SERVES 2

A recipe by Heather and Alexis Wallis. Parents will love it, too!

8 ounces penne pasta

1 tablespoon butter

½ cup ketchup

½ cup shredded Cheddar
cheese

Cook pasta according to package directions. Drain and place in a saucepan. Add butter, mixing until melted. Add ketchup and cheese and mix until cheese starts to melt. Serve hot.

OPTIONAL: Sprinkle with toasted pine nuts.

Spaghetti Bolognese

SERVES 4

1 pound thin spaghetti

1 pound lean ground beef

2 cups pasta sauce with
mushrooms or onions

1 cup shaved Parmesan
cheese

Cook the pasta according to package directions. Meanwhile, in a skillet, cook beef and 2 tablespoons water over medium heat until beef is no longer pink. Stir in pasta sauce, reduce the heat, cover, and cook for 6 minutes. Drain pasta and place equal portions of pasta in 4 bowls. Top with sauce. Sprinkle with cheese to finish.

Sweet Crumbed Chicken

SERVES 6

Recipe from Cyndi O'Meara. These are a real hit!

2 cups cornflakes, ground

1 cup grated Parmesan cheese

¾ cup plain yogurt

6 skinless, boneless chicken breast halves (6 ounces each)

Preheat the oven to 350°F. Line a baking sheet with parchment paper. Combine cornflakes and cheese in a bowl. Place yogurt in another bowl. Coat chicken with yogurt and then with cornflake and cheese mixture. Bake for 20 minutes, or until just cooked through.

OPTIONAL: Cut breasts into tenderloins and reduce the baking time.

Too Easy Chicken Nuggets

SERVES 2

These are requested at least twice a week!

¾ pound skinless, boneless chicken breasts, cut into bite-size pieces

1½ cups mayonnaise

1½ cups bread crumbs

1 tablespoon butter, melted

Preheat the oven to 350°F. Line a baking sheet with parchment paper. Coat chicken with mayonnaise and roll in bread crumbs. Place on baking sheet. Drizzle with a little butter and bake for 20 minutes.

Tuna with Spaghetti
SERVES 2

A recipe from the lovely Alice Beattie!

1 can (12 ounces) tuna chunks, drained

1 can (14.7 ounces) SpaghettiOs

½ cup grated cheese (your favorite)

½ cup bread crumbs

Preheat the oven to 350°F. Combine tuna and SpaghettiOs. Place in a baking dish and sprinkle with cheese and bread crumbs. Bake for 15 to 20 minutes, or until the cheese is golden and bubbling.

Vegetable Shapes
SERVES 2

These put a thrill into eating vegetables!

1 potato

4-ounce piece butternut squash

2 tablespoons olive oil

Preheat the oven to 350°F. Line a baking sheet with parchment paper. Cut potato and squash into ¾-inch-thick slices. Use cookie cutters (stars, hearts, animal shapes, etc.) to cut out as many shapes as possible. Coat with olive oil and place on a baking sheet. Bake for 15 to 20 minutes, turning halfway through.

OPTIONAL: Keep scraps and make mashed potato and squash on another night.

SWEETS

He who teaches children learns more than they do.
—German proverb

Apricot Dream Balls

MAKES 24

Paul Bermingham's favorite!!!

¾ cup mixed dried fruit

¼ cup dried apricots

1 tablespoon coconut milk

1 cup shredded coconut

Put mixed fruit, apricots, and coconut milk in a food processor, and whiz until the mixture comes together. Shape into balls and roll in coconut. Chill until firm.

OPTIONAL: We have used condensed milk and tahini instead of coconut milk, and both were yummy.

Baked Custard

SERVES 4

A recipe from our much-loved "Grandma," Jennette McCosker.

2 cups milk

2 tablespoons sugar

½ teaspoon vanilla extract

2 eggs, beaten

Preheat the oven to 300°F. In a saucepan, bring milk and sugar to a boil, stirring occasionally. Add vanilla and remove from the heat. Stirring constantly, pour about ¼ cup of hot milk mixture into eggs. This warms the eggs and prevents curdling. Pour the warmed egg mixture into the remaining milk mixture. Stir briskly until well combined. Pour into a small baking dish. Place the dish in a larger pan and pour in hot water to come halfway up the sides of the custard. Bake for about 1 hour.

OPTIONAL: Sprinkle with nutmeg prior to baking.

Banana Chips

These are terrific as a lunch box snack.

4 bananas

Preheat the oven to 425°F. Peel and thinly slice bananas. Bake on a baking sheet lined with parchment paper for 15 to 20 minutes, or until crisp.

TIP: If you are like Errol McCosker (Kim's dad), dry your own fruit with a dehydrator. His dried mango is simply divine and his grandchildren love it!

Blancmange

SERVES 4

A recipe from Jocelyn Wilson.

1 can (12 ounces) evaporated milk

1 cup chopped strawberries

2 tablespoons honey

1 envelope gelatin

Mix milk, strawberries, and honey together. Dissolve the gelatin in 3 tablespoons warm water, stirring vigorously until smooth. Add to the mixture, stirring well. Pour into individual bowls. Allow to set in the fridge for a couple of hours.

OPTIONAL: Substitute 1 cup chocolate topping for the strawberries.

Caramelized Bananas with Ice Cream

SERVES 2

2 tablespoons butter

2 finger or mini bananas

1 tablespoon sugar

2 scoops vanilla ice cream

Preheat a heavy skillet and melt butter. Add bananas and sprinkle with sugar. Cook for 1 minute. Turn and cook for another minute, or until they reach desired doneness. Serve each with a scoop of ice cream.

Chocolate Balls

MAKES ABOUT 30

A recipe loved by Matthew, Brady, and Harry McCosker.

- 14 ounces graham crackers, crushed
- 3 tablespoons unsweetened cocoa powder
- 1 can (14 ounces) condensed milk
- ½ cup shredded coconut

Mix crushed graham crackers, cocoa, and condensed milk together to make a sticky consistency. Using a generous teaspoon of mixture, roll into balls, then cover with coconut. Chill before serving.

TIP: These can also be frozen.

Chocolate Nut Clusters

MAKES 24

- ¼ cup unsalted pistachios
- ¼ cup slivered almonds
- 14 ounces milk chocolate
- ½ cup golden raisins

Line a baking sheet with parchment paper. Heat a small heavy skillet, add pistachios and almonds, and cook, stirring constantly, until browned lightly (take care not to scorch nuts, because they burn easily). Remove nuts from the hot pan. Melt chocolate in the microwave, stirring every 15 seconds. Stir nuts and raisins into chocolate. Scoop out the chocolate mixture by heaping tablespoons and drop onto the baking sheet. Refrigerate clusters, uncovered, until set.

Chocolate-Dipped Fruit

SERVES 4

Makes a nice platter at kids' parties.

17 ounces milk chocolate

2 bananas, thickly sliced

1 cup strawberries

¾ cup dried apricots

Line a baking sheet with parchment paper. Melt chocolate in the microwave, stirring every 15 seconds. Dip fruit, one piece at a time, into chocolate to coat about three-fourths of each piece of fruit. Place fruit in a single layer on the baking sheet, and refrigerate until set.

Crunchy Banana on a Stick

SERVES 2

These are nutritious and delicious!!

1 banana, halved lengthwise

½ cup banana or vanilla yogurt

½ cup crushed crunchy cookies (any will do, as long as they're crunchy)

Thread each banana half onto a small wooden skewer. Spread with some yogurt and roll in cookie crumbs.

Fluffy Pudding

SERVES 4

A recipe from the lovely Gwen Colyer.
Our children adore this, and it is so easy!!

1 box (3 ounces)
gelatin dessert
(your favorite flavor)

1 can (12 ounces)
evaporated milk, chilled

Dissolve gelatin in 1 cup boiling water, let cool, and add evaporated milk. Beat until really frothy. Place in the fridge until set.

OPTIONAL: Serve with whatever fruit complements the flavor of the gelatin.

Frozen Fruit Treats

SERVES 4 TO 6

1 cup strawberries

1 cup canned crushed
pineapple

2 bananas

1 cup orange or apple juice

Combine all ingredients in a blender and process until smooth. Pour into a Popsicle mold or small paper cups and freeze. Serve partially defrosted, with a spoon if in a cup, or fully frozen if in a stick mold.

Fruit Kebabs

SERVES 4 TO 6

Recipe from Jen Whittington.

Choice of 2 fruits: berries, melon, citrus (whatever you have in the fridge or in the fruit basket)

6 ounces fruit yogurt

1 tablespoon honey

Dice fruit into bite-size pieces (skin and clean, where required). Thread the chosen fruits alternately onto a skewer, leaving enough room at the base so the skewer can be held. Drizzle with yogurt and honey.

Homemade Krispies Squares

MAKES 16

2½ cups Rice Krispies

½ cup colored sprinkles

1½ cups marshmallows, chopped

½ cup (1 stick) butter, melted, plus a little extra for pan

Mix Rice Krispies, sprinkles, and half the marshmallows in a bowl. In a small saucepan, melt remaining marshmallows. Add butter and mix well. Pour mixture over ingredients, combining well. Pour into a greased 9-inch square pan and pat down. Place in fridge to set. Remove, cut, and serve.

Honey Joys

MAKES 12

Aussie kids for decades have grown up with these.

3 tablespoons butter

⅓ cup sugar

1 tablespoon honey

4 cups cornflakes

Preheat the oven to 300°F. Heat butter, sugar, and honey in a small saucepan until frothy. Remove from the heat. Add cornflakes and mix well. Spoon into a muffin tin lined with paper cases and bake for 10 minutes.

Jelly Snow

SERVES 4 TO 6

1 box (3 ounces)
   gelatin dessert
   (your favorite flavor)

1 cup frozen berries (any type), partially thawed

2 cups vanilla ice cream

Make gelatin dessert according to package directions and leave until almost set. Blend with a handheld mixer or blender—it becomes frothy and pale. Leave to set completely. Serve with "purple ice cream" made by mixing berries into ice cream.

Marshmallow Medley

SERVES 4

Another little treasure from Aine Watkins.

12 marshmallows, chopped

¼ cup sour cream

4 tangerines, peeled, separated into segments, and seeded

1½ tablespoons shredded coconut

Mix all ingredients together, chill, and serve.

Mini Muffins

MAKES 12

You will be surprised at how quick and easy these are.

1 cup self-rising flour, sifted

1 cup heavy cream

3 tablespoons sugar

½ cup blueberries

Preheat the oven to 350°F. Grease a mini muffin tin. Combine all ingredients until just blended. Spoon mixture into muffin cups. Bake for 10 minutes, or until golden.

TIP: Overbeating muffin batter prevents a healthy rise.

Prune Snow

SERVES 4

Remembered as a favorite from Kim's childhood!

1 cup pitted prunes

2 egg whites

2 tablespoons superfine sugar

Place prunes in a saucepan and cover with water. Cook for about 10 minutes, or until soft. Remove from the heat, drain, and let cool. Meanwhile, beat egg whites until fluffy. Add sugar, bit by bit, and continue to beat until stiff. Mash prunes. Fold egg whites into prunes.

OPTIONAL: Use the egg yolks to make a yummy creamy custard to serve with it.

Rice Pudding

SERVES 4

A recipe from the beautiful Mary Moore.

4 cups milk

½ cup medium-grain rice

2 tablespoons sugar

½ teaspoon vanilla extract

Preheat the oven to 300°F. Add all ingredients to a 9-inch square baking dish and bake in the middle of the oven for 1½ hours.

Sesame & Honey Bars

MAKES 12

*These are made in a couple of minutes
and are really tasty.*

1 cup sesame seeds

1 cup old-fashioned rolled
oats

½ cup honey

½ cup (1 stick) butter

Preheat the oven to 350°F. Grind sesame seeds and oats together in a food processor. Melt honey and butter in a small saucepan, then pour mixture into the food processor. Blend and turn out into a rectangular baking dish lined with parchment paper. Bake for 20 to 25 minutes, or until golden brown. Cut the bars in the dish and then leave them to cool.

Snickers Slice

SERVES 8

Fabulous energy booster in a lunch box.

3 Snickers bars

¼ cup (½ stick) butter, plus a
little extra for greasing

4 cups Rice Krispies

In a microwaveable dish, melt Snickers bars and butter for a couple of minutes, stirring every 30 seconds, or until melted. Add Rice Krispies and mix well. Press into a lightly greased baking pan and refrigerate. Cut into slices when ready to serve.

Summer Yogurt Treat

SERVES 1

½ banana, sliced

½ cup grapes, halved

2 tablespoons yogurt

½ cup fruit muesli, toasted

Place fruit in a glass bowl. Top with yogurt and sprinkle with fruit muesli.

Sweet Carrot Snacks

SERVES 2 TO 4

Great for after school.

4 chilled carrots

2 tablespoons honey

1 teaspoon sesame seeds

Peel chilled carrots, halve lengthwise, then slice crosswise into four pieces. Combine honey and sesame seeds in a small bowl for dipping.

OPTIONAL: You can also use tahini as a substitute for honey. A nutritious and healthy snack.

Sweet Toasted Sandwich

SERVES 4

A great idea from Meredith Mullally.

1 tablespoon butter

8 slices raisin bread

1 can (21 ounces)
   apple pie filling

1 teaspoon cinnamon sugar

Butter bread and turn 4 slices buttered side down. Thickly coat these 4 slices with apple filling and sprinkle with cinnamon sugar. Place remaining 4 slices of bread, buttered side up, on the apples. Toast as you would a normal grilled sandwich.

OPTIONAL: Serve plain or with ice cream.

Toffees

MAKES 12

2 cups sugar

1 tablespoon vinegar

Colored sprinkles

In a heavy-bottomed saucepan, combine sugar, 1 cup water, and vinegar. Stir over medium heat until sugar has completely dissolved. Bring to a boil, reduce the heat slightly, and boil without stirring for 20 minutes (it is ready when a drop of the mixture in cold water hardens). Pour into mini muffin cases and decorate with sprinkles. Leave to set at room temperature.

FOR THE LUNCH BOX

Anyone who thinks the art of conversation is dead
ought to tell a child to go to bed!!!
—Robert Gallagher

A healthy school lunch box is something we moms try to aim for every day. The best lunch is one that's nutritious and quick to prepare, but also fun and easy to eat. Encouraging your children to be involved in choosing foods and preparing their lunch can help ensure that it not only gets eaten, but is enjoyed as well.

Fresh Fruit and Vegetables

If you shop wisely and choose fruit in season, you can still afford these and many more fresh fruits and vegetables for lunch boxes.

FRUIT

Apples: Ask the vendor for the crunchiest varieties, as no one, least of all a child, likes a mealy apple! The skin of an apple is the best part, nutrientwise.

Apricots

Asian pears: Crunchy and juicy—our children love these.

Bananas

Grapes: Green, red, or purple. The darker the skin, the more antioxidants!

Kiwifruit

Mangoes: Get lots in season and freeze for use all year.

Nectarines

Oranges, quartered

Peaches

Pears

Pineapple chunks

Plums

Strawberries

Tangerines

Watermelon, honeydew melon, or cantaloupe, cubed

VEGETABLES

Bell pepper, yellow, red, or green, cut into strips

Carrot sticks

Celery sticks

Cherry tomatoes

Cucumbers, cut into strips

Green beans, whole

Sugar snap peas and snow peas

Dairy

You read everywhere that experts suggest you include one serving of dairy food in a lunch box every day. One serving is equal to:

1 cup milk: In the summer, try freezing milk overnight. Wrap the container in a cloth for the lunch box to minimize sweating. By lunchtime it will be ready to drink.

1½ ounces cheese slices, cubes, or sticks

1 cup yogurt—plain or with fruit: Try freezing a container of yogurt and placing it in the lunch box. As with the milk, by lunchtime it will have partially thawed and be ready to eat.

Protein Food

Choose one or more of these protein-rich foods as a starter for your sandwich:

Baked beans: Choose low salt where available. Consider trying
 Mexican or barbecue flavors.
Bean salad
Canned fish, such as tuna, salmon, sardines, or mackerel
Cheese
Deviled eggs
Falafel
Fish sticks
Homemade lentil patties
Peanut butter
Plain unsalted nuts (⅓ cup)
Sliced cold meats or fish, such as ham, turkey, smoked salmon,
 chicken, lamb, corned beef, roast beef, ham, meat loaf, or
 meatballs

Sandwiches

Try to include lots of varieties of bread, fillings, and spreads to retain interest in sandwiches. Breads/rolls: whole wheat, multigrain, rye, corn, pita, sourdough, pumpernickel, mountain, lavash, white fiber-enriched, omega-3-enriched, soy and flax, herb . . . The list goes on.

Pack sandwich fillings separately so that children can make their own sandwiches once they sit down to eat. This should prevent any "It's too soggy!" complaints.

Bagels
Crackers

Crispbreads

English muffins

Foccacias

Mountain bread: Try wheat, corn, rice, or barley

Pita bread

Raisin bread

Rice cakes

Scones

Super Sandwich Ideas Gathered from Some "Super Mommies" in Our Lives!

1. Roast beef, tomato, grainy mustard, and shredded iceberg lettuce
2. Peanut butter and mashed banana
3. Peanut butter and bean sprouts (sounds unusual but is really tasty!)
4. Banana on raisin bread
5. Cheese with grated carrot, lettuce, and golden raisins
6. Tuna and tomato
7. Baked beans on a roll
8. Chicken, chopped celery, walnuts, and a dash of mayo
9. Cottage cheese mixed with chopped apple and dates (yummo!)
10. Ham, chutney, lettuce, grated carrot, and grated cheese on a foccacia
11. Egg and lettuce
12. Apple and cream cheese
13. Salmon mixed with cream cheese to bind
14. Cheese and tomato
15. Ham and cheese
16. Cream cheese, chopped celery, and golden raisins
17. Peanut butter and grated carrot

18. Leftover roast meat with grated carrot, chopped lettuce, and chutney
19. Tuna, lettuce, and ketchup
20. Ham, cheese, and a pineapple ring (Make sure the pineapple is dry before placing it on the sandwich.)
21. Mashed banana
22. Grated carrot, cheese, and mayonnaise
23. Curried egg salad

A MORE EXCITING SANDWICH

Triple Deckers: These are really easy and really fun. Make a sandwich with 3 slices of bread and two layers of filling. Remove the crusts and cut the sandwich into three strips.

Pita Pockets: Fill a pita with your choice of filling: lean meat, salad, egg, grated cheese, carrot, etc.

Cut-out Shapes: Buy different cookie cutters to make bread shapes for your toddlers (use the excess for bread crumbs to avoid waste). It is fun for them to eat a shark-shaped sandwich!!

FOOD SAFETY AND HYGIENE TIPS FOR LUNCH BOXES

1. Use an insulated lunch box or carry bag.
2. Use a frozen ice brick or drink bottle in the lunch box.
3. Freeze sandwiches the night before both as a timesaver and to keep foods cool.
4. Chill cooked foods, e.g., hard-boiled egg, before packing in the lunch box.
5. Store lunch box in a cool spot.
6. Wash little (and big) hands thoroughly before eating, and after going to the toilet or playing with pets.
7. Wash lunch box thoroughly after school every day.

A RECIPE FOR ALL MOTHERS

Today I left some dishes dirty,
The bed I made at 3:30
The nappies soaked a little longer,
The odor grew a little stronger.
The crumbs I spilt the day before
Are staring at me from the floor.
The fingerprints, there on the wall
Will likely still be there, next fall.
The dirty streaks on the window panes
Will still be there next time it rains.
"Shame on you old lazy-bones," I say
"And just what have you done, today?"

I nursed a baby till he slept,
I held a toddler while he wept.
I played a game of hide and seek
I squeezed a toy, so it would squeak.
I pulled a wagon, sang a song,
Taught a child right from wrong.
What did I do this whole day through?
Not much that shows, I guess it's true . . .
Unless you think that what I've done
Might be important to someone
With bright blue eyes and soft blond hair.
If that is true, I've done my share.

—JOANNE GREEN

DRINKS

Be fabulous!

—Kim McCosker

Apple, Carrot & Ginger Juice

SERVES 1

A great breakfast drink!

2 Granny Smith apples

2 carrots

1 tablespoon coarsely chopped fresh ginger

Don't peel before blending or juicing, as most of the vitamins are found just beneath the skin. Serve with a little crushed ice.

Apple, Celery & Carrot Juice

MAKES 1 CUP

2 Granny Smith apples

2 celery stalks, strings removed

2 carrots

Blend or juice.

Banana & Maple Supreme

MAKES 1 CUP

½ cup chilled milk

1 banana

2 teaspoons maple syrup

Blend together with a couple of ice cubes and serve immediately.

Banana Lassi

MAKES 2 CUPS

1 large banana

1 cup plain yogurt

½ cup milk

1 tablespoon sugar

Combine all ingredients in a blender and blend until smooth.

Citrus & Strawberry Frappé

MAKES 2 CUPS

This is a great "fresh start to the day" drink.

2 oranges, peeled and quartered

1 lemon, peeled and quartered

1 cup strawberries

Pick out seeds from oranges and lemon. Combine orange and lemon in a blender with strawberries and 1 cup of ice and blend.

Energizer Drink

MAKES 2 CUPS

1 ripe banana

½ cup fresh or frozen berries (strawberries, raspberries, or mixed berries)

½ cup milk

¼ cup natural yogurt

Combine all ingredients in a blender and blend until smooth. Add ½ cup ice for a frappé. Serve in a tall glass.

Grape Melon Drink

MAKES 2 TO 3 CUPS

2 cups watermelon chunks

2 cups seedless grapes

Blend or juice both watermelon and grapes with 6 ice cubes for a light, refreshing drink.

Homemade Lemonade

MAKES 4 CUPS

1 cup superfine sugar

1 cup lemon juice

3 cups sparkling water or seltzer, chilled

In a saucepan, combine sugar and 1 cup tap water and stir over low heat until the sugar dissolves. Allow to cool. Stir in lemon juice. To serve, top with chilled sparkling water and lots of crushed ice.

Melon Delight

MAKES 1 CUP

¾ cup pineapple juice

4 slices honeydew melon

1 teaspoon honey

1 spring mint

In a blender, blend pineapple juice, melon, and honey with ½ cup ice. Pour into a large glass. Serve garnished with fresh mint leaves.

Minty Apple Iced Tea

MAKES 4 CUPS

3 peppermint tea bags

2 cups apple juice

8 mint leaves, torn

1 small apple, thinly sliced

Soak tea bags in 2 cups boiling water and let stand for 10 minutes. Discard the bags. Pour tea into a pitcher, and mix in juice and mint. Cover with plastic wrap and chill for 1 hour before serving. Add apple slices, stir, and serve in tall glasses with plenty of ice.

Orange & Yogurt Shake

MAKES 3 CUPS

2 large oranges, peeled

1 cup plain Greek yogurt

1 teaspoon honey

Combine oranges, yogurt, and honey in a blender and process until smooth.

Peanut, Pineapple & Banana Shake

MAKES 4 CUPS

2 cups plain yogurt

2 frozen bananas

2 cups chilled pineapple pieces (canned or fresh)

½ cup peanut butter

Combine all ingredients in a blender and process until smooth.

Pineapple & Mint Icy

MAKES 2 CUPS

1 pineapple, peeled and chopped

5 sprigs fresh mint, leaves only

Combine pineapple and mint in a blender and process until smooth. Serve over loads of crushed ice.

Piña Colada Shake

MAKES 4 CUPS

Recipe from Cyndi O'Meara.

2 cups pineapple cubes

1 cup coconut milk

2 bananas

1 cup ice

Combine all ingredients in a blender and process until smooth. Serve chilled.

Punch

MAKES 3¾ QUARTS

1 can (12 ounces) frozen orange juice concentrate, reconstituted

1 can (46 ounces) pineapple juice

2 quarts clear soda (club soda, ginger ale, lemon-lime, etc.)

In a large punch bowl, combine the orange juice and pineapple juice. Add the soda.

OPTIONAL: To give the punch a nice rosy hue, use raspberry ginger ale.

TIP: To keep the punch nice and cold, freeze water in a ring mold and float the ice ring in the punch bowl.

Strawberry Punch

SERVES 6 TO 8

1 can (6 ounces) frozen
lemonade concentrate

10 ounces frozen
strawberries, thawed

1 pint lemon-lime sherbet

1 quart ginger ale

Prepare lemonade and chill. Combine all
ingredients just before serving and mix
until sherbet is dissolved.

> **TIP:** To keep the punch nice and cold, freeze water in a
> ring mold and float the ice ring in the punch bowl.

Strawberry Smoothie

MAKES 4 CUPS

1 cup chilled unsweetened
apple juice

2 frozen bananas

1 scoop vanilla ice cream

1 pint chilled strawberries

Combine all ingredients in a blender and
process until smooth. Serve chilled.

GREAT COMBINATION MEALS

Beef

1. Massaman Curry (116), jasmine rice topped with cashew nuts, Crunchy Snow Peas (97)
2. Pesto-Stuffed Steaks (117), Mushroom Risotto (171), arugula, Oven-Baked Tomatoes (101)
3. Quick Meat Loaf (119), mixed green salad, Balsamic and Garlic Dressing (69)
4. Easy Roast Beef (114) or Garlic Roast Beef (115) with Horseradish Cream (46), seasoned roast vegetables, hearty homemade bread

Chicken

1. Chicken, Butternut, and Chickpea Curry (125), Fluffy Rice Without a Cooker (83), yogurt, pappadums
2. Cheese and Prosciutto Chicken (124), sweet potato, baby spinach
3. Cajun Chicken kebabs (124), spinach and strawberry salad, Chili Mayonnaise (41)
4. Mascarpone and Cilantro Chicken (133), Garlic Potatoes (84), mixed green salad, Balsamic and Garlic Dressing (69).

Fish

1. Baked Salmon with Pesto Crust (139), polenta, spinach, shaved Parmesan, marinated olives
2. Herb-baked fish fillets, Sautéed Lemon Potatoes (89), Asparagus with Balsamic Dressing (92)
3. Moroccan salmon, Antipasto Tarts (53), Hummus (25), arugula
4. Pasta with Crab and Lemon Cream Sauce (157), green salad, Vinaigrette (80), garlic bread

Lamb

1. Lamb Shank Casserole (153), Mashed Potato with Pine Nuts (85), seasoned roast vegetables
2. Asian-Style Lamb Chops (152), Onion Jam (48), tempura-battered vegetables (104)
3. Tandoori Lamb (154), Greek yogurt, Avocado Salsa (39)
4. Lamb and bacon parcels, mixed salad, Balsamic and Garlic Dressing (69)

Pork

1. Pork and Coconut Satay Sticks (162), Sweet Potato Oven Fries (90), mixed green salad
2. Pork and Bacon Wraps (161), Brie Bruschetta (17), olive oil, fresh basil
3. Rich Tomato Pork (163), Oven-Roasted Wedges (86), Beans with Garlic and Pine Nuts (94)
4. Roast Pork (164), grilled pears, Grilled Corn with Parmesan and Cayenne (99), gravy

Vegetarian

1. Sour Cream Quiche (172), green salad with Creamy Salad Dressing (73)
2. Green Bean Curry (169), Fluffy Rice Without a Cooker (83), yogurt, pappadums
3. Pasta with Tomato and Basil (171), Brie Bruschetta (with or without tomatoes) (17)
4. Mushroom Risotto (171), shaved Parmesan, Oven-Baked Tomatoes (101), arugula, asparagus

HANDY HOME TIPS

This book has morphed into an all-purpose household manual over the years. Here follow some terrific little tips, gathered from some of our nearest and dearest.

Alleviate discomfort when plucking your eyebrows: Smooth baby teething gel over the area to numb the pain.

Band-Aids: Removing them is easy if you soak a cotton ball in baby oil and rub it over the tape.

Blender: Cleaning your blender is much easier if you fill it about a third of the way with hot water, add a couple of drops of your dishwasher detergent, and then turn it on!

Cooking pasta: Add about 8 cups of water to a large pot. One tablespoon of salt should be added to the water as it begins to boil. If the salt is added too soon it can give off an odor, which can affect the taste of the pasta. If it is added immediately before the pasta, the salt may not have enough time to completely dissolve in the water. The salt helps bring out the flavor in the pasta and helps it hold its shape.

Brittle and flaking fingernails: Mix 2 level teaspoons of gelatin into half a glass of fruit juice or cold water. Drink at once and repeat daily for at least 6 weeks. You should see a dramatic improvement in your nails after about 2 months.

Brittle nails: To avoid, massage cod liver oil, which is rich in vitamin A, into cuticles and nails. After 3 months, nails will be stronger and cuticles smoother.

Broken glass: Use a piece of bread to pick up the fragments of broken glass.

Brunette or red hair: To add shine, after shampooing rinse with freshly brewed black coffee that you have let cool, followed by cold water.

Carry a water bottle with you at all times: Water flushes toxins in the body and also fills you up.

Celery: Prevent celery from wilting by wrapping it in foil before putting it in the refrigerator, and it will keep for weeks.

Chewing gum in children's hair: Dab with a cloth soaked with eucalyptus oil. Gum should come out without tears.

Cockroaches: To repel, mix equal parts borax and sugar and place where cockroaches gather, e.g., under the fridge and dishwasher.

Disinfectant: Tea tree oil, added to cleaners or in the rinsing water, is a natural disinfectant.

Drains of your sink: To clean, put 1 tablespoon of baking soda down the sink followed by 2 tablespoons of vinegar, and let stand for 15 minutes, then flush with hot water.

Eyes: Relax your eyes at regular intervals when reading or using a computer by taking 5-minute breaks, or focusing at a distance of 5 yards away.

Fabric interior of your car: Use baby wipes to remove marks. Even the long-term stains will come off. Really!

Fish: It generally takes 10 minutes per inch of thickness to cook fish. To be sure it doesn't overcook, start checking the fish at 7 to 8 minutes.

Flowers: Cut an inch off the bottom of the stems and place in water within 13 seconds (prevents inhalation of air). Adding a little bleach to the water will preserve your flowers longer, because the water is cleaner. Change the water regularly.

Fridges and freezers: To keep them smelling fresh, sprinkle a few drops of vanilla extract onto a damp cloth and wipe the interior walls and shelves. To dispel odors, place a small container of baking soda inside the fridge.

For an instant face-lift: Beat an egg white and apply it to your skin. Leave on for about 10 minutes and rinse off. Your skin will be tighter and appear firmer.

Green hair: Remove the green tinge from your hair (the result of swimming in chlorinated water) by washing your hair in 5 aspirin tablets dissolved in ⅓ cup of shampoo. Alternatively, put 3 tablespoons of vinegar in your shampoo.

Housework: Hire help or barter for help. If you can't afford a weekly cleaner, employ someone to do the heavy cleaning once a month. Work this into your budget; it is worth every cent because of the exhilarating feeling that walking into a clean house offers!!

Iron: To clean the soleplate, wipe it with a cloth soaked in cold tea. This will remove stains immediately.

Leather furniture: To clean, wash it with warm, soapy water using a nail brush and cloth. Allow to dry, then coat the cleaned area with Vaseline; rub it in with a cloth to get the residue off. This works better than most expensive cleaners. To revive, polish it with linseed oil and vinegar in a proportion of 1:2.

Lower back pain: To relieve, sleep with a pillow under your knees to take the pressure off your lower back and have a good night's sleep.

Make-do hair spray: Getting ready for a big night out and realize you're out of hair spray? Try dissolving 1 tablespoon of sugar in a glass of hot water, wait until it cools, and then put it into a spray bottle. It's effective and environmentally friendly, too!

Mascara: As it gets older and starts to dry up, soak in a mug of hot water before using.

Meat: Remove meat from the fridge about an hour before grilling. Your meat will be more succulent as a result.

Minimize redness of acne on your face: Soak a cotton ball in eye-drops and hold on the spot for 20 seconds.

Moths: Repel pantry moths by keeping an open packet of Epsom salts on the shelf.

Nail polish: It will last longer if you keep it in the fridge.

Nice-smelling car: Place a roll of fabric softener sheets under the seats (apple and lavender are particularly nice). The diversity and staying power of the scents are great and they work better than expensive car deodorizers.

Nicotine stains on fingers: Remove by rubbing with nail polish remover or by simply giving up smoking!!

Oven: Reduce the unpleasant smell left from oven cleaners by baking some citrus peelings on low heat.

Oven cleaning: To reduce the need, line the bottom of your oven with foil cut to size. The foil catches drips and grease and can be easily replaced when dirty.

Pearls: To clean your pearls, shake them in a bag of uncooked rice.

Puffy eyes 1: Soak 2 tea bags, then put them in the freezer for a few minutes, place on your eyes, lie back, and relax! Or grate a raw potato, mold it into a mushy pack, and put it on your eyes and lids for 10 to 20 minutes. The potato starch will help smooth the eye-area skin and ease away puffiness.

Puffy eyes 2: Try using some cold cucumber slices on your eyes at the end of the night to relieve tired eyes. An oldie, but a goodie.

Razor burn: Avoid razor burn after shaving your legs by moisturizing beforehand. While shaving cream is the most popular method, try prepping your leg with hair conditioner for a few minutes before shaving. It will hold moisture on the leg longer and provide a very smooth shave.

Remove baked-on stains from glass baking dishes: Soak them in a strong solution of borax and water.

Removing mascara: A cheap and effective way to do this is to use baby oil. Simply dip a Q-tip in, or cover a cotton ball with, baby oil and gently wipe over your lashes. The oil will also soften the skin around your eyes, so there is no need for eye creams, either.

Revitalizing eye gel: Keep your eye gel in the fridge to really soothe tired eyes or cool you down on a hot day.

Self-rising flour: To make, mix together 2¼ pounds all-purpose flour, 2 tablespoons baking soda, and ¼ cup cream of tartar. Sift well.

Sharp lip line and eye line: Put your eyeliner or lipliner pencil in the freezer briefly before sharpening to get a fine point.

Spaghetti: When cooking, add 1 teaspoon of cooking oil or 1 teaspoon of butter to the water in rice, noodles, or spaghetti. This will prevent the water from boiling over and the grains or strands from sticking together.

Stainless steel sink: To brighten, use a damp cloth soaked in vinegar.

Steak cooking times (depending on thickness):
Rare: 2 to 5 minutes
Medium: 8 to 12 minutes
Well done: 12 to 15 minutes

Strawberries: Purchase strawberries that are red all over. The redder near the hull of the fruit, the sweeter.

Stuck-on food in pots, pans, and baking dishes: Fill the pan with water and place a fabric softener sheet in the water. Allow the pan to soak overnight. The food will wipe right out!

Swollen hands: If you have a ring stuck on your finger because your fingers have swollen, soak your hand in ice water until the ring slips off.

Take the generic brand of prescriptions: Generics often come from the same company and are exactly the same as the full-priced version.

Tie a small bell to any door leading out of the house: You'll be able to hear a small child making his or her escape!

Washing clothes: Hang clothes as soon as you can after washing to reduce creasing.

When giving distasteful medicine to young children: First, run an ice cube over the child's tongue to temporarily freeze the taste buds.

When starting a new fitness regimen: Don't overcommit yourself, as you will soon lose interest. Start with a little activity and increase as your fitness level does.

When traveling with a baby: Take some baking soda with you in a small ziplock bag. Should your baby be sick, simply sprinkle clothes with the soda. Brush off when dry, and the odor will have disappeared.

Whiten your fingernail tips: Soak your nails in lemon juice.

Wood floors: Floors that have been sealed can be cleaned with cold tea on a mop. A little vinegar in the bucket of water with the detergent helps to remove any grease from kitchen floors.

INVITATION

To all who have contributed a recipe in this book by way of e-mail, mail, or phone, we would like to extend our sincerest thanks. Your suggestions have been invaluable.

If *you* have a 4 Ingredient recipe and think others would enjoy cooking it, please visit us on our Facebook page. We'd love to meet you! Join us for our weekly online cooking school, where you will see us making some of our fabulous 4 Ingredient recipes. You will be super surprised at just how easy they are! We also share hints on how to save time and money in the kitchen, *and* you even have a chance to win some great prizes.

Visit us at facebook.com/4Ingredients.

Thank you and happy cooking!

Kim & Rachael

ACKNOWLEDGMENTS

Personal thanks from Kim

There are so many people to thank who have made 4 *Ingredients* what it has gone on to become. But along the journey there are those that are . . . consistent. Rach, you are an amazing woman and I am blessed to have you in my life. Jennette, my mum—if I can be half the mum you are to me, then I will be a brilliant mum, too. Melinda, please don't ever leave me; you are my glue! And to the absolute LOVES OF MY LIFE: my husband, Glen, and my three beautiful boys, Morgan, Hamilton, and Flynn. You bring more happiness and love into my life than should be legal! All I do, I do for you!

Personal thanks from Rachael

Kim, THANK YOU so very much for sharing your idea with me, and I am thrilled that I was able to help you bring it to reality. Your passion, energy, and commitment are outstanding and admirable to all who are blessed to come into your life. To Paul, for his support and eagerness in taste testing—I could not have done this without you. To my gorgeous, BEAUTIFUL little boys—Jaxson and my baby twins, Bowie and Casey—you are my inspiration and motivation to be better and do better; I truly hope that I am building a legacy that you can be proud of, and I love you with every cell of my spirit. And to my darling brother, "Spud," a very talented chef whose guidance in constructing this book has been invaluable. THANK YOU!

INDEX

ABOUT THE AUTHORS

Rachael Bermingham is the energetic, dynamic, and proud mum of Jaxson and six-month-old twin boys, Bowie and Casey. She has written six bestselling books in the last four years and is regarded as one of Australia's number one female authors. Rachael wrote two bestselling books, *Read My Lips* and *How to Write Your Own Book and Make It a Bestseller,* before lending her writing and marketing talent to join with Kim to write the phenomenally successful *4 Ingredients* cookbooks. She travels the world as a motivational speaker and mentor and is the founder of Bermingham Books, a mentoring and book distribution center for authors wanting to know how to write, produce, and promote their own books.

When Rachael's not working or whipping up something fabulous in the kitchen, she can be found "chillaxing" at home with friends and family and soaking up the sun, surf, and sand of the beautiful Sunshine Coast in Australia.

Kim McCosker is the proud mother of three boys (Morgan, eight; Hamilton, five; and Flynn, two), the lady who had the idea and who is now the coauthor of the internationally bestselling 4 Ingredients series, which includes *4 Ingredients, 4 Ingredients 2,* and *4 Ingredients Gluten Free.* Kim completed a Bachelor of International Finance and worked for several years in the finance industry before finally resigning to spend time raising her beautiful boys.

For Kim, family is the *most important thing* in the world, and with the loving support of her wonderful husband, Glen, she has been able to juggle the demands of a busy work life around her treasured home life. Life presents many opportunities, but having the courage and the time to pursue them in what is an ever-increasingly busy and demanding world is hard. She is living proof that you can achieve whatever you want in life with a *great idea* and *lots of HARD WORK!*